FIRST
LIGHT

FIRST LIGHT

Mother & Son Poems

A Twentieth-Century American Selection

EDITED BY

JASON SHINDER

A Harvest / HBJ Original

Harcourt Brace Jovanovich, Publishers

San Diego   New York   London

The epigraph is excerpted from "Canto LXXXI,"
from *The Cantos of Ezra Pound*. Copyright 1948 by Ezra Pound.
Reprinted by permission of New Directions Publishing Corporation.

Library of Congress Cataloging-in-Publication Data
First light: mother & son poems: a twentieth-century
American selection/edited by Jason Shinder.
p. cm.
ISBN 0-15-631136-4
1. Mothers and sons — Poetry. 2. American
poetry — 20th century. I. Shinder, Jason, 1955 —
PS595.M66F57   1992
811'.50803520431 — dc20   92-3781

Printed in the United States of America
Designed by Camilla Filancia
First edition   A B C D E

for my mother,

EDITH SHINDER

What thou lovest well remains,
                                the rest is dross
What thou lov'st well shall not be reft from thee
What thou lov'st well is thy true heritage

EZRA POUND

Contents

The mother-son poems in this selection were written over the last nine decades in various places and in many states of mind. They seem to have emerged not out of a poet's conscious decision to write a "mother-son" poem but rather out of each poet's almost helpless need to understand this primary relationship, whether beautiful or painful, real or imagined.

As I reread these poems, they often seem to be illuminated by something deeper, beyond the poet's need for greater understanding. I imagine the source of this illumination to be the very first feeling of love between a mother and a son — the first light, so to speak. It is an elusive and ephemeral light, one that may shine briefly when a poet tries to capture the mother-son relationship in language.

The birth of a son, the death of a son, or the death of a mother — these are catalysts for many of the poems. In addition, the difficult but rewarding task of mothers and sons simply learning to live together has produced a wealth of poems — poems that seem to be saying: So far, so good (or not so good) between us; now we need to try and go the distance. The results in both cases are often poems of the highest qualities of honesty and affection.

In my house, the words exchanged between my mother and me were conditioned mostly by the habits and accidents of the day. The words changed some when an intense joy or sorrow inspired us to speak, in our different fashions, about the feelings we had for each other and for life, which we usually kept unexamined and hidden inside.

As I grew older, it became clearer and clearer that I wanted the dialogue between my mother and myself to be far deeper. I wanted to express my many feelings for her — love, concern, disappointment, frustration, and anger. Yet it was (and still is) difficult to initiate such a dialogue. I felt that voicing some of these feelings would be too unfamiliar and, therefore, too unsettling. I was afraid such a dialogue might create a distance instead of bringing us closer.

Poetry helped. In many poems on the subject, I discovered immediate companionship. I felt linked to other sons and mothers in their efforts to speak honestly to each other. And I found that the poems helped me to imagine — and begin to develop — better communication and understanding between my mother and me.

First Light is the first book to present poetry exclusively by American mothers and sons on the mother and son relationship. The poets are arranged chronologically. Multiple poems by a single poet are arranged in the order of their publication, when such information was available. Thus the reader may follow the lines of development of the mother-son poetry of individual poets as well as trace the development of the theme in twentieth-century American poetry.

In any collection, the question of choice naturally surfaces. The poems I have selected represent a very small part of a larger body of work. Because of space constraints, I have limited the collection to shorter mother-son poems and to sections, where appropriate, of longer poems on the subject. I can only say that I hope *First Light* contains poems that readers will want to return to again and again for pleasure, to explore the larger issues of the self, and to help sustain our commitments to one another, to our families, and to our work.

The truth is that one can see in poems only what one can see in oneself. I am grateful, therefore, to those people who provided new insights into the poems I was considering for this collection, and to the many poets, editors, teachers, and friends who brought mother-son poems to my attention.

Thanks to Arlene Hellerman and Annie Markovich for their help in securing the necessary permissions, and to Cynthia Sosland for her comments regarding the introduction. Thanks also to the book's editors, Claire Wachtel and Ruth Greenstein, for their support, patience, and good counsel. Very special thanks to Sophie Cabot Black for her concern and her insights, and to Samuel Kashner and Steven Bauer as well. And, finally, thanks to my sister, Nina, and brother, Martin, for their support and special understanding.

Examining the mother-son relationship, and the possibilities for greater understanding and intimacy such examination affords, demands candor, compassion, and forgiveness. These are the qualities I think we would find if we could reduce the poems in this collection to their barest elements.

JASON SHINDER
1992

FIRST
LIGHT

Wallace Stevens

IN THE CAROLINAS

The lilacs wither in the Carolinas.
Already the butterflies flutter above the cabins.
Already the new-born children interpret love
In the voices of mothers.

Timeless mother,
How is it that your aspic nipples
For once vent honey?

The pine-tree sweetens my body.
The white iris beautifies me.

Wallace Stevens

WORLD WITHOUT PECULIARITY

The day is great and strong—
But his father was strong, that lies now
In the poverty of dirt.

Nothing could be more hushed than the way
The moon moves toward the night.
But what his mother was returns and cries on his breast.

The red ripeness of round leaves is thick
With the spices of red summer.
But she that he loved turns cold at his light touch.

What good is it that the earth is justified,
That it is complete, that it is an end,
That it in itself is enough?

It is the earth itself that is humanity . . .
He is the inhuman son and she,
She is the fateful mother, whom he does not know.

She is the day, the walk of the moon
Among the breathless spices and, sometimes,
He, too, is human and difference disappears

And the poverty of dirt, the thing upon his breast,
The hating woman, the meaningless place,
Become a single being, sure and true.

William Carlos Williams

THE HORSE SHOW

Constantly near you, I never in my entire
sixty-four years knew you so well as yesterday
or half so well. We talked. You were never
so lucid, so disengaged from all exigencies
of place and time. We talked of ourselves,
intimately, a thing never heard of between us.
How long have we waited? Almost a hundred years.

You said, Unless there is some spark, some
spirit we keep within ourselves, life, a
continuing life's impossible — and it is all
we have. There is no other life, only the one.
The world of the spirits that comes afterward
is the same as our own, just like you sitting
there they come and talk to me, just the same.

They come to bother us. Why? I said. I don't
know. Perhaps to find out what we are doing.
Jealous, do you think? I don't know. I
don't know why they should want to come back.
I was reading about some men who had been
buried under a mountain, I said to her, and
one of them came back after two months,

digging himself out. It was in Switzerland,
you remember? Of course I remember. The
villagers tho't it was a ghost coming down
to complain. They were frightened. They

do come, she said, what you call
my "visions." I talk to them just as I
am talking to you. I see them plainly.

Oh if I could only read! You don't know
what adjustments I have made. All
I can do is to try to live over again
what I knew when your brother and you
were children — but I can't always succeed.
Tell me about the horse show. I have
been waiting all week to hear about it.

Mother darling, I wasn't able to get away.
Oh that's too bad. It was just a show;
they make the horses walk up and down
to judge them by their form. Oh is that
all? I tho't it was something else. Oh
they jump and run too. I wish you had been
there, I was so interested to hear about it.

from *Vi Va*

XLIII

if there are any heavens my mother will (all by herself) **have**
one. It will not be a pansy heaven nor
a fragile heaven of lilies-of-the-valley but
it will be a heaven of blackred roses

my father will be (deep like a rose
tall like a rose)

standing near my

swaying over her
(silent)
with eyes which are really petals and see

nothing with the face of a poet really which
is a flower and not a face with
hands
which whisper
This is my beloved my

                     (suddenly in sunlight
he will bow,

& the whole garden will bow)

LAMENT

Listen, children:
Your father is dead.
From his old coats
I'll make you little jackets;
I'll make you little trousers
From his old pants.
There'll be in his pockets
Things he used to put there,
Keys and pennies
Covered with tobacco;
Dan shall have the pennies
To save in his bank;
Anne shall have the keys
To make a pretty noise with.
Life must go on,
And the dead be forgotten;
Life must go on,
Though good men die;
Anne, eat your breakfast;
Dan, take your medicine;
Life must go on;
I forget just why.

AND FOR HIS MOTHER

For your own mother, you remain Baby
jumping to give her (crumpled in crumpled fist)
a baby dandelion, green and gold.
But, as now and again, when tipsy friends plumb deeps
of conversation unexpressed, you came
to hover over the home-brew, and then spoke
in random piano notes some fellow made
to ornament his wit. Your mild eyes gleamed
    with scorn to beg for an immortal selfhood
    and warm blood, humming underneath cool skin
    clear as October evening, flooded all
    your vernal frailty with fury. Streams
    of sympathy pour over distant height
    dispassionately intimate in death.

Meridel Le Sueur

BUDDED WITH CHILD

Before your cry
   I never heard a cry,
Headless ghost I rode the prairies,
The bodyless head screaming after me.
Skeleton, I searched for rose and flesh,
Lamenting in bereaved villages
Howling in stone cities
I gave berries to strangers
I gave them fruits
   I gave them fruits
For stones and bones and broken words.
In the place where crying begins
The place of borders, the place of the enemy
I begot you, child
Before you I did not know flowers
   out of snow,
Or milk of meadows out of drouth.
Before your cry I never heard a cry,
Or globular breast and milk without summons.
Exiled I cried along the rivers
   caged in time and loss,
Empty pod I longed for winged seeds.
Till merged in earth's agony of birth
   leapt bridge
   struck lyre
Impaled on earth and fleshes spring,
   budded with child.

Before you child I never knew the breast of milk
the arm of love
the kerneled grain of groats
Before your face I never saw a face descending
down my belly to time's horizon
breast and skin multiplied into multitude
and benevolence.

Gwendolyn B. Bennett

SECRET

I shall make a song like your hair . . .
Gold-woven with shadows green-tinged,
And I shall play with my song
As my fingers might play with your hair.
Deep in my heart
I shall play with my song of you,
Gently. . . .
I shall laugh
At its sensitive lustre . . .
I shall wrap my song in a blanket,
Blue like your eyes are blue
With tiny shots of silver.
I shall wrap it caressingly,
Tenderly. . . .
I shall sing a lullaby
To the song I have made
Of your hair and eyes . . .
And you will never know
that deep in my heart
I shelter a song for you
Secretly. . . .

MOTHER TO SON

Well, son, I'll tell you:
Life for me ain't been no crystal stair.
It's had tacks in it,
And splinters,
And boards torn up,
And places with no carpets on the floor —
Bare.
But all the time
I'se been a-climbin' on,
And reachin' landin's,
And turnin' corners,
And sometimes goin' in the dark
Where there ain't been no light.
So boy, don't you turn back.
Don't you set down on the steps
'Cause you finds it kinder hard.
Don't you fall now —
For I'se still goin', honey,
I'se still climbin',
And life for me ain't been no crystal stair.

BLACK BABY

The baby I hold in my arms is a black baby.
    Today I set him in the sun and
    Sunbeams danced on his head.
The baby I hold in my arms is a black baby.
    I toil, and I cannot always cuddle him.
    I place him on the ground at my feet.
    He presses the warm earth with his hands,
    He lifts the sand and laughs to see
    It flow through his chubby fingers.
    I watch to discern which are his hands,
    Which is the sand. . . .
Lo . . . the rich loam is black like his hands.

The baby I hold in my arms is a black baby.
    Today the coal-man brought me coal.
    Sixteen dollars a ton is the price I pay for coal. —
    Costly fuel . . . though they say: —
    Men must sweat and toil to dig it from the ground.
    Costly fuel . . . 'Tis said: —
    If it is buried deep enough and lies hidden long enough
    'Twill be no longer coal but diamonds. . . .
    My black baby looks at me.
    His eyes are like coals,
    They shine like diamonds.

DELIA REXROTH

California rolls into
Sleepy summer, and the air
Is full of the bitter sweet
Smoke of the grass fires burning
On the San Francisco hills.
Flesh burns so, and the pyramids
Likewise, and the burning stars.
Tired tonight, in a city
Of parvenus, in the inhuman
West, in the most blood drenched year,
I took down a book of poems
That you used to like, that you
Used to sing music I
Never found anywhere again —
Michael Field's book, *Long Ago*.
Indeed it's long ago now —
Your bronze hair and svelte body
I guess you were a fierce love,
A wild wife, an animal
Mother. And now life has cost
Me more years, though much less pain,
Than you had to pay for it.
And I have bought back, for and from
Myself, these poems and paintings,
Carved from the protesting bone,
The precious consequences
Of your torn and distraught life.

Stanley Kunitz

THE PORTRAIT

My mother never forgave my father
for killing himself,
especially at such an awkward time
and in a public park,
that spring
when I was waiting to be born.
She locked his name
in her deepest cabinet
and would not let him out,
though I could hear him thumping.
When I came down from the attic
with the pastel portrait in my hand
of a long-lipped stranger
with a brave mustache
and deep brown level eyes,
she ripped it into shreds
without a single word
and slapped me hard.
In my sixty-fourth year
I can feel my cheek
still burning.

ALL THE LITTLE ANIMALS

"You are not pregnant," said the man
with the probe and the white white coat;
"Yes she is," said all the little animals.
Then the great gynecologist examined. "You are not now, and
I doubt that you ever have been," he said with authority.
"Test me again." He looked at his nurse and shrugged.
"Yes she is," said all the little animals, and laid down their
lives for my son and me.
Twenty-one years later, my son a grown man and far away at
the other ocean,
I hear them : "Yes you are," say all the little animals.
I see them, they move in great jumping procession through my
waking hours,
those frogs and rabbits look at me with their round eyes, they
kick powerfully with their strong hind legs,
they lay down their lives in silence,
all the rabbits saying Yes, all the frogs saying Yes,
in the face of all men and all institutions,
all the doctors, all the parents, all the worldly friends, all the
psychiatrists, all the abortionists, all the lawyers.
The little animals whom I bless and praise and thank forever,
they are part of my living,
go leap through my waking and my sleep, go leap through my
life and my birth-giving and my death,
go leap through my dreams,
and my son's life
and whatever streams from him.

Robert Hayden

THE WHIPPING

The old woman across the way
   is whipping the boy again
and shouting to the neighborhood
   her goodness and his wrongs.

Wildly he crashes through elephant ears,
   pleads in dusty zinnias,
while she in spite of crippling fat
   pursues and corners him.

She strikes and strikes the shrilly circling
   boy till the stick breaks
in her hand. His tears are rainy weather
   to woundlike memories:

My head gripped in bony vise
   of knees, the writhing struggle
to wrench free, the blows, the fear
   worse than blows that hateful

Words could bring, the face that I
   no longer knew or loved. . . .
Well, it is over now, it is over
   and the boy sobs in his room,

And the woman leans muttering against
   a tree, exhausted, purged —
avenged in part for lifelong hidings
   she has had to bear.

Delmore Schwartz

A YOUNG CHILD AND
HIS PREGNANT MOTHER

At four years Nature is mountainous,
Mysterious, and submarine. Even

A city child knows this, hearing the subway's
Rumor underground. Between the grate,

Dropping his penny, he learned out all loss,
The irretrievable cent of fate,

And now this newest of the mysteries,
Confronts his honest and studious eyes —

His mother much too fat and absentminded,
Gazing far past his face, careless of him,

His fume, his charm, his bedtime, and warm milk
As soon the night will be too dark, the spring

Too late, desire strange, and time too fast,
This first estrangement is a gradual thing

(His mother once so svelte, so often sick!
Towering father did this: what a trick!)

Explained too cautiously, containing fear,
Another being's being, becoming dear:

All men are enemies: thus even brothers
Can separate each other from their mothers!

No better example than this unborn brother
Shall teach him of his exile from his mother,

Measured by his distance from the sky,
Spoken in two vowels,
                    I am I.

2ND WIND

My son's house
    Up on our hill,
Looks out, over my shoulder;
Its barn-cabin being
    Takes to a scudding wind.

It looks away at land
    Roiling under white cover, —
Tree-banks massive as dinosaurs
Smoothing to field; snow-squalls.
    Drummed by a wild wind

I look up at
    This edifice tuned
By twenty years green
Learning. Across the valley
    An iron flurry speaks.

As my son's house
    Looks far, it is
Seasoned, there; from this proud
Young life a seconding
    Wind breathes through me —

And I accept
    My autumn wandering,
Winter, June's
Skeleton summer . . . Now
    So blows, now, my 2nd wind!

THE TRUTH

When I was four my father went to Scotland.
They *said* he went to Scotland.

When I woke up I think I thought that I was dreaming —
I was so little then that I thought dreams
Are in the room with you, like the cinema.
That's why you don't dream when it's still light —
They pull the shades down when it is, so you can sleep.
I thought that then, but that's not right.
Really it's in your head.

And it was light then — light at *night*.
I heard Stalky bark outside.
But really it was Mother crying —
She coughed so hard she cried.
She kept shaking Sister,
She shook her and shook her.
I thought Sister had had her nightmare.
But he wasn't barking, he had died.
There was dirt all over Sister.
It was all streaks, like mud. I cried.
She didn't, but she was older.
                              I thought she didn't
Because she was older, I thought Stalky had just gone.
I got *everything* wrong.
I didn't get one single thing right.
It seems to me that I'd have thought
It didn't happen, like a dream,

Except that it was light. At night.
They burnt our house down, they burnt down London.
Next day my mother cried all day, and after that
She said to me when she would come to see me:
"Your father has gone away to Scotland.
He will be back after the war."

The war then was different from the war now.
The war now is *nothing*.

I used to live in London till they burnt it.
What was it like? It was just like here.
No, that's the truth.
My mother would come here, some, but she would cry.
She said to Miss Elise, "He's not himself";

She said, "Don't you love me anymore at all?"
I was *myself*.
Finally she wouldn't come at all.
She never said one thing my father said, or Sister.
Sometimes she did,
Sometimes she was the same, but that was when I dreamed it.
I could tell I was dreaming, she was just the same.

That Christmas she bought me a toy dog.

I asked her what was its name, and when she didn't know
I asked her over, and when she didn't know
I said, "You're not my mother, you're not my mother.
She *hasn't* gone to Scotland, she is dead!"
And she said, "Yes, he's dead, he's dead!"
And cried and cried; she *was* my mother,
She put her arms around me and we cried.

John Berryman

from *THE DREAM SONGS*
1 2 9

Thin as a sheet his mother came to him
during the screaming evenings after he did it,
touched F.J.'s dead hand.
The parlour was dark, he was the first pall-bearer in,
he gave himself a dare & then did it,
the thing was quite unplanned,

riots for Henry the unstructured dead,
his older playmate fouled, reaching for him
and never will he be free
from the older boy who died by the cottonwood
& now is to be planted, wise & slim,
as part of Henry's history.

Christ waits. That boy was good beyond his years,
he served at Mass like Henry, he never did
one extreme thing wrong
but tender his cold hand, latent with Henry's fears
to Henry's shocking touch, whereat he fled
and woke screaming, young & strong.

David Ignatow

from *SHADOWING THE GROUND*
3 4

Mother, how wrinkled and old must you become
before you die? How many foolish things
out of your agony must you say? In your prime
you commanded us and without prompting
we lived with you. When we were of age
we departed. In your old age, weakened
of command, reduced to complaining, you are
not the same person, and we are not the same
for it either. We too see ourselves alone,
for with love and command gone we are directed
towards ourselves, and alone now we are lonely
with everyone.

A LOUD SONG, MOTHER

for my son, Daniel Seymour

My son is five years old and tonight he sang this song to me.
He said, it's a loud song, Mother, block up your ears a little, he
said wait I must get my voice ready first. Then tunelessly
but with a bursting beat he chanted from his room enormously,
> strangers in my name
> strangers all around me
> strangers all over the world
> strangers running on stars
A deafening declaration this jubilant shout of grief
that trumpets final fellowship and flutes a whole belief.
Alone and in the dark he clears his throat to yawp his truth
that each living human creature's name is Ruth.
He sings a world of strangers running on the burning stars
a race on every-colored feet with freshly calloused scars.

Our stark still strangers waited back of doors and under beds
their socket eyes stared at us out of closets; in our heads.
We crawled on hob-nailed knees across our wasted starless land
each smugly thinking his the only face that wore a brand.
Sons, may you starve the maggot fears that ate our spirit's meat
and stride with brother strangers in your seven-league bare feet.

THE RONDANINI PIETÀ

His face seems blinded
with pain
       & dazed into
anonymity,
         but she —
woman-mother-beloved & loving
is giving birth to him still,
                 he issues (still)
from her body,
         they are
of the same flesh,
            pressed
together
     & only her touch,
the complete giving,
           the flow of
her body into his can heal him.
                  She knows that
& dimly, in his pain,
          he knows it
also,
   as the earth,
   with its leaves,
   its streams
its branches, might
heal a deer
that has been wounded,
        so she, the mother,
        pours forth all the power of

her life-streams
                into him,
seems to warm him,
                to melt, in
the heat of compassion
                what is
wounded in him,
                to take to
herself the pain,
                to dissolve & become
one with it,
                hide it inside herself,
fill her own flesh with it
                & perhaps, taking it into herself
change it,
                as branches
filled with a storm can
make a space that is
windless
                beneath them.

R o b e r t   L o w e l l

SAILING HOME
FROM RAPALLO
   (February 1954)

Your nurse could only speak Italian,
but after twenty minutes I could imagine your final week,
and tears ran down my cheeks. . . .

When I embarked from Italy with my Mother's body,
the whole shoreline of the *Golfo di Genova*
was breaking into fiery flower.
The crazy yellow and azure sea-sleds
blasting like jack-hammers across
the *spumante*-bubbling wake of our liner,
recalled the clashing colors of my Ford.
Mother travelled first-class in the hold
her *Risorgimento* black and gold casket
was like Napoleon's at the *Invalides*. . . .

While the passengers were tanning
on the Mediterranean in deck-chairs,
our family cemetery in Dunbarton
lay under the White Mountains
in the sub-zero weather.
The graveyard's soil was changing to stone —
so many of its deaths had been midwinter.
Dour and dark against the blinding snowdrifts,
its black brook and fir trunks were as smooth as masts.
A fence of iron spear-hafts
black-bordered its mostly Colonial grave-slates.

The only "unhistoric" soul to come here
was Father, now buried beneath his recent
unweathered pink-veined slice of marble.
Even the Latin of his Lowell motto:
Occasionem cognosce,
seemed too businesslike and pushing here,
where the burning cold illuminated
the hewn inscriptions of Mother's relatives:
twenty or thirty Winslows and Starks.
Frost had given their names a diamond edge. . . .

In the grandiloquent lettering on Mother's coffin,
Lowell had been misspelled *LOVEL.*
The corpse
was wrapped like *panettone* in Italian tinfoil.

LETTER TO AN ABSENT SON

It's right to call you son. That cursing alcoholic
is the god I married early before I really knew him:
spiked to his crossbeam bed, I've lasted thirty years.
Nails are my habit now. Without them I'm afraid.

At night I spider up the wall to hide in crevices
deeper than guilt. His hot breath smokes me out.
I fall and fall into the arms I bargained for
sifting them cool as rain. A flower touch could tame me.

Bring me down that giant beam to lie submissive
in his fumbling clutch. One touch. Bad weather
moves indoors: a cyclone takes me.

How shall I find a shelter in the clouds, driven by
gods, gold breaking out of them everywhere?
Nothing is what it pretends. It gathers to a loss
of leaves and graves. Winter in the breath.
Your father looked like you, his dying proportioned
oddly to my breast. I boxed him in my plain pine
arms and let him take his ease just for a minute.

from *M O T H E R*

7 T H E   D E A T H

On the sea of motherhood and death you voyaged, waif
     of eternity,
You were the pioneer whether you knew it or not,
You were the unwitting pioneer, and most of the time unwilling,
You who for seventy years despised your stepfather, I am certain
     (in the nature of things) with justice,
You who knowingly first met your father when you were thirty,
The seedy businessman from St. Louis, that droll city,
You whose husband, loving and incapable, the knight in podgy
     armor, the poet from the land of the Brownies,
Talking away your blues with the wisdom he gave instead of love
     and that he himself could never use,
(Oh, might I say, with the dicky bird, that things past redress
     are now with me past care!),
You, my mother, who taught me without words that no secret
     is better kept than the one everybody guesses,
I see you now in your eternal moment that has become mine,
You twisted, contorted, your agonized bones,
You whom I recognize forever, you in the double exposure,
You in the boat of your confinement lying,
Drifting on the sea as the currents and long winds take you,
Penitent for the crime committed against you, victim of your own
     innocence,
(Existence is the crime against the existing),
Drifting, drifting in the uncaused universe that has no right to be.

THE SON

I   THE DISCLOSURE
He-who-came-forth was
it turned out
a man —

Moves among us from room to room of our life
in boots, in jeans, in a cloak of flame
pulled out of his pocket along with
old candywrappers, where it had lain
transferred from pants to pants,
folded small as a curl of dust,
from the beginning —

unfurled now.

The fine flame
almost unseen in common light.

II   THE WOODBLOCK
He cuts into a slab of wood,
engrossed, violently precise.
Thus, yesterday, the day before yesterday,
engines of fantasy were evolved
in poster paints. Tonight
a face forms under the knife,

slashed with stern
crisscrosses of longing, downstrokes
of silence endured—
                              his visioned
own face!—
down which from one eye

rolls a tear.
              His own face
drawn from the wood,

deep in the manhood his childhood
so swiftly led to, a small brook rock-leaping
into the rapt, imperious, seagoing river.

James Dickey

A BIRTH

Inventing a story with grass,
I find a young horse deep inside it.
I cannot nail wires around him;
My fence posts fail to be solid,

And he is free, strangely, without me.
With his head still browsing the greenness,
He walks slowly out of the pasture
To enter the sun of his story.

My mind freed of its own creature,
I find myself deep in my life
In a room with my child and my mother,
When I feel the sun climbing my shoulder

Change, to include a new horse.

FOR MARGARET

My mother near her death
is white as a downy feather.
I used to think her death was as distant
as a tropical bird,
a giant macaw, whatever that is —
a thing I have as little to do with
as the distant poor.
I find a single feather of her suffering,
I blow it gently as she blew
into my neck and ear.

A single downy feather is on the scales,
opposed of things of weight, not spirit.
I remember the smell of burning feathers.
I wish we could sit upon the grass
and talk about grandchildren
and great-grandchildren.
A worm directs us into the ground.
We look alike.

I sing a lullaby to her about her children,
who are safe, and their children.
I place a Venetian lace tablecloth
on the grass of the whitest linen.
The wind comes with its song
about things given that are taken away
and given again in another form.

Why are the poor cawing, hooting,
screaming in the woods?
I wish death were a whippoorwill.
Why is everything so heavy?
I did not think
she was still helping me carry
the weight of my life.
Now the world's poor are before me.
How can I lift them one by one in my arms?

James Merrill

from *UP AND DOWN*
THE EMERALD

Hearing that on Sunday I would leave,
My mother asked if we might drive downtown.
Why certainly — off with my dressing gown!
The weather had turned fair. *We* were alive.

Only the gentle General she married
Late, for both an old way out of harm's,
Fought for breath, surrendered in her arms,
With military honors now lay buried.

That week the arcana of his medicine chest
Had been disposed of, and his clothes. Gold belt
Buckle and the letter from President Roosevelt
Went to an unknown grandchild in the West.

Downtown, his widow raised her parasol
Against the Lenten sun's not yet detectable
Malignant atomies which an electric needle
Unfreckles from her soft skin each fall.

Hence too her chiffon scarf, pale violet,
And spangle-paste dark glasses. Each spring we number
The new dead. Above ground, who can remember
Her as she once was? Even I forget,

Fail to attend her, seem impervious . . .
Meanwhile we have made through a dense shimmy
Of parked cars burnished by the midday chamois
For Mutual Trust. Here cool gloom welcomes us,

And all, director, guard, quite palpably
Adore her. Spinster tellers one by one
Darting from cages, sniffing to meet her son,
Think of her having a son — ! She holds the key

Whereby palatial bronze gates shut like jaws
On our descent into this inmost vault.
The keeper bends his baldness to consult,
Brings a tin box painted mud-brown, withdraws.

She opens it. Security. Will. Deed.
Rummages further. Rustle of tissue, a sprung
Lid. Her face gone queerly lit, fair, young,
Like faces of our dear ones who have died.

No rhinestone now, no dilute amethyst,
But of the first water, linking star to pang,
Teardrop to fire, my father's kisses hang
In lipless concentration round her wrist.

Gray are these temple-drummers who once more
Would rouse her, girl-bride jeweled in his grave.
Instead, she next picks out a ring. "He gave
Me this when you were born. Here, take it for —

For when you marry. For your bride. It's yours."
A den of greenest light, it grows, shrinks, glows,
Hermetic stanza bedded in the prose
Of the last thirty semiprecious years.

I do not tell her, it would sound theatrical,
Indeed this green room's mine, my very life.
We are each other's; there will be no wife;
The little feet that patter here are metrical.

But onto her worn knuckle slip the ring.
Wear it for me, I silently entreat,
Until — until the time comes. Our eyes meet.
The world beneath the world is brightening.

Robert Creeley

MOTHER'S VOICE

In these few years
since her death I hear
mother's voice say
under my own, I won't
want any more of that.
My cheekbones resonate
with her emphasis. Nothing
of not wanting only

but the distance there from
common fact of others
frightens me. I look out
at all this demanding world

and try to put it quietly back,
from me, say, thank you,
I've already had some
though I haven't

and would like to
but I've said no, she has,
it's not my own voice anymore.
It's higher as hers was

and accommodates too simply
its frustrations when
I at least think I want more
and must have it.

Allen Ginsberg

from *KADDISH*
for Naomi Ginsberg, 1894–1956

III
Only to have not forgotten the beginning in which she drank
cheap sodas in the morgues of Newark,
only to have seen her weeping on grey tables in long wards of her
universe
only to have known the weird ideas of Hitler at the door, the
wires in her head, the three big sticks
rammed down her back, the voices in the ceiling shrieking out
her ugly early lays for 30 years,
only to have seen the time-jumps, memory lapse, the crash of
wars, the roar and silence of a vast electric shock,
only to have seen her painting crude pictures of Elevateds
running over the rooftops of the Bronx
her brothers dead in Riverside or Russia, her lone in Long Island
writing a last letter—and her image in the sunlight at the
window
"The key is in the sunlight at the window in the bars the key is
in the sunlight,"
only to have come to that dark night on iron bed by stroke when
the sun gone down on Long Island
and the vast Atlantic roars outside the great call of Being to its
own
to come back out of the Nightmare—divided creation—with her
head lain on a pillow of the hospital to die
—in one last glimpse—all Earth one everlasting Light in the
familiar blackout—no tears for this vision—

But that the key should be left behind — at the window — the key
    in the sunlight — to the living — that can take
that slice of light in hand — and turn the door — and look back
    see
Creation glistening backwards to the same grave, size of universe,
size of the tick of the hospital's clock on the archway over the
    white door —

         I V
O mother
what have I left out
O mother
what have I forgotten
O mother
farewell
with a long black shoe
farewell
with Communist Party and a broken stocking
farewell
with six dark hairs on the wen of your breast
farewell
with your old dress and a long black beard around the vagina
farewell
with your sagging belly
with your fear of Hitler
with your mouth of bad short stories
with your fingers of rotten mandolines
with your arms of fat Paterson porches
with your belly of strikes and smokestacks
with your chin of Trotsky and the Spanish War
with your voice singing for the decaying overbroken workers
with your nose of bad lay with your nose of the smell of the
    pickles of Newark

with your eyes
with your eyes of Russia
with your eyes of no money
with your eyes of false China
with your eyes of Aunt Elanor
with your eyes of starving India
with your eyes pissing in the park
with your eyes of America taking a fall
with your eyes of your failure at the piano
with your eyes of your relatives in California
with your eyes of Ma Rainey dying in an ambulance
with your eyes of Czechoslovakia attacked by robots
with your eyes going to painting class at night in the Bronx
with your eyes of the killer Grandma you see on the horizon from
    the Fire-Escape
with your eyes running naked out of the apartment screaming
    into the hall
with your eyes being led away by policemen to an ambulance
with your eyes strapped down on the operating table
with your eyes with the pancreas removed
with your eyes of appendix operation
with your eyes of abortion
with your eyes of ovaries removed
with your eyes of shock
with your eyes of lobotomy
with your eyes of divorce
with your eyes of stroke
with your eyes alone
with your eyes
with your eyes
with your Death full of Flowers

V

Caw caw caw crows shriek in the white sun over grave stones in
  Long Island

Lord Lord Lord Naomi underneath this grass my halflife and my
  own as hers

caw caw my eye be buried in the same Ground where I stand in
  Angel

Lord Lord great Eye that stares on All and moves in a black cloud

caw caw strange cry of Beings flung up into sky over the waving
  trees

Lord Lord O Grinder of giant Beyonds my voice in a boundless
  field in Sheol

Caw caw the call of Time rent out of foot and wing an instant in
  the universe

Lord Lord an echo in the sky the wind through ragged leaves the
  roar of memory

caw caw all years my birth a dream caw caw New York the bus
  the broken shoe the vast highschool caw caw all Visions of
  the Lord

Lord Lord Lord caw caw caw Lord Lord Lord caw caw caw Lord

Frank O'Hara

TO MY MOTHER

Oh witness! to be sure,
you are gone in your violet sleeve,
and I am riding in a grey car
through the suburbs of my nose.

Have you escaped your impatience?
I am guilty and the sky is blue
as a restaurant full of tapioca.
And isn't it ordinary?

like the many famous things
that are called "stuff" somewhere
and are on maps with their bloody veins,
I mean, highways somewhere.

Have you escaped yet? if you
haven't I hope you've killed someone,
or suicide's grown curious of someone,
or someone's accidentally died.

Galway Kinnell

THE LAST HIDING
PLACES OF SNOW

1

The burnt tongue
fluttered, "I'm dying . . ."
and then, "Why did . . . ? Why . . . ?"
What earthly knowledge did she still need
just then, when
the tongue failed
or began speaking in another direction?

Only the struggle for breath
remained: groans made
of all the goodbyes ever spoken all
turned meaningless; surplus world sucked back
into a body laboring to live
all the way to death; and past death, if it must.

There is a place in the woods
where you can hear
such sounds: sighs, groans
seeming to come
from the darkness of spruce boughs,
from glimmer-at-night of the white birches,
from the last hiding places of snow,

a breeze,
that's all, driving
across certain obstructions: every stump

speaks,
the spruce needles play out of the air
the sorrows cried into it somewhere else.

Once in a while, passing the place,
I have imagined I heard
my old mother calling, thinking out loud her
mother-love toward me, over those many miles
from where her bones lie,
five years
in earth now, with my father's thirty-years' bones.

I have always felt
anointed by her love, its light
like sunlight
falling through broken panes
onto the floor
of a deserted house: we may go, it remains,
telling of goodness of being, of permanence.

So lighted I have believed
I could wander anywhere,
among any foulnesses, any contagions,
I could climb through the entire empty world
and find my way back and learn again to be happy.

But when I've stopped and listened,
all I've heard was
what may once have been speech
or groans, now
shredded to a hiss from passing
through the whole valley of spruce needles.

My mother did not want me to be born;
afterwards, all her life, she needed me to return.
When this more-than-love flowed toward me, it brought
    darkness;
she wanted me as burial earth wants — to heap itself gently upon
    but also to annihilate —
and I knew, whenever I felt longings to go back,
that is what wanting to die is. That is why

dread lives in me,
dread which comes when what gives life beckons toward death,
dread which throws through me
waves
of utter strangeness, which wash the entire world empty.

2

I was not at her bedside
that final day, I did not grant her ancient,
huge-knuckled hand
its last wish, I did not let it
gradually become empty of the son's hand — and so
hand her, with more steadiness, into the future.
Instead, old age took her
by force, though with the help
of her old, broken attachments
which had broken
only on this side of death
but had kept intact on the other.

I would know myself lucky if my own children
could be at my deathbed, to take
my hand in theirs and with theirs
to bless me back into the world as I leave,
with smoothness pressed into roughness,
with folding-light fresh runner hands to runner of wasted breath,
with mortal touch whose mercy two bundled-up figures greeting
    on a freezing morning, exposing the ribboned ends of right
    arms, entwining these, squeeze back and forth before walking
    on,
with memories these hands keep, of strolling down Bethune
    Street in spring, a little creature hanging from each arm, by a
    hand so small it can do no more than press its tiny thumb
    pathetically into the soft beneath my thumb . . .

But for my own mother I was not there . . .
and at the gates of the world, therefore, between
holy ground
and ground of almost all its holiness gone, I loiter
in stupid fantasies I can live that day again.

Why did you come so late?
Why will you go too early?

I know now there are regrets
we can never be rid of;
permanent remorse. Knowing this, I know also
I am to draw from that surplus stored up
of tenderness which was hers by right,
which no one ever gave her,
and give it away, freely.

3

A child, a little girl,

in violet hat, blue scarf, green sweater, yellow skirt, orange socks,
    red boots,
on a rope swing, swings
in sunlight
over a garden in Ireland, backfalls,
backrises,
forthsinks,
forthsoars, her charmed life holding its breath
innocent of groans, beyond any
future, far past the past: into a pure present.

Now she wears rhythmically into the air
of morning
the rainbow's curve, but upside down
so that angels may see
beloved dross promising heaven:
no matter what fire we invent to destroy us,
ours will have been the brightest world ever existing . . .
The vision breaks,
the child suddenly grows old, she dies . . .

Every so often, when I look
at the dark sky, I know she remains
among the old endless blue lightedness
of stars; or finding myself out in a field
in November, when a strange
starry perhaps first snowfall blows
down across the darkening air, lightly,
I know she is there, where snow

falls flakes down fragile softly
falling until I can't see the world
any longer, only its stilled shapes.

Philip Levine

SOLOING

My mother tells me she dreamed
of John Coltrane, a young Trane
playing his music with such joy
and contained energy and rage
she could not hold back her tears.
And sitting awake now, her hands
crossed in her lap, the tears start
in her blind eyes. The TV set
behind is gray, expressionless.
It is late, the neighbors quiet,
even the city — Los Angeles — quiet.
I have driven for hours down 99,
over the Grapevine into heaven
to be here. I place my left hand
on her shoulder, and she smiles.
What a world, a mother and son
finding solace in California
just where we were told it would
be, among the palm trees and all-
night super markets pushing orange
back-lighted oranges at 2 A.M.
"He was alone," she says, and does
not say, just as I am, "soloing."
What a world, a great man half
her age comes to my mother
in sleep to give her the gift
of song, which — shaking the tears
away — she passes on to me, for now

I can hear the music of the world
in the silence and that word:
soloing. What a world — when I
arrived the great bowl of mountains
was hidden in a cloud of exhaust,
the sea spread out like a carpet
of oil, the roses I had brought
from Fresno browned on the seat
beside me, and I could have
turned back and lost the music.

Adrienne Rich

JERUSALEM

In my dream, children
are stoning other children
with blackened carob-pods
I dream my son is riding
on an old grey mare
to a half-dead war
on a dead-grey road
through the cactus and thistles
and dried brook-beds.

In my dream, children
are swaddled in smoke
and their uncut hair smolders
even here, here
where trees have no shade
and rocks have no shadow
trees have no memories
only the stones and
the hairs of the head.

I dream his hair is growing
and has never been shorn
from slender temples hanging
like curls of barbed wire
and his first beard is growing
smoldering like fire
his beard is smoke and fire
and I dream him riding
patiently to the war.

What I dream of the city
is how hard it is to leave
and how useless to walk
outside the blasted walls
picking up the shells
from a half-dead war
and I wake up in tears
and hear the sirens screaming
and the carob-tree is bare.

Adrienne Rich

THIS

Face flashing free   child-arms
lifting the collie pup
torn paper on the path
Central Park   April '72
behind you   minimal
those benches and that shade
that brilliant light in which
you laughed longhaired
and I'm the keeper of
this little piece of paper
this little piece of truth

I wanted this from you —
laughter   a child turning
into a boy   at ease
in the spring light   with friends
I wanted this for you

I could mutter   *Give back*
that day   give me again
that child   with the chance
of making it all right
I could yell   *Give back that light*
on the dog's teeth   the child's hair
but no rough drafts are granted
— Do you think I don't remember?

did you think I was all-powerful
unimpaired   unappalled?
yes   you needed that from me
I wanted this from you

Etheridge Knight

REPORT TO THE MOTHER

Well, things / be / pretty bad now, Mother —
Got very little to eat.
The kids got no shoes for their tiny feet.
Been fighting with my woman, and one / other
Woe: — Ain't got a cent to pay the rent.

Been oiling / up / my pistol too —
Tho I / be / down with the flu,
So what / are / You going to do . . . ?

O Mother don't sing me
To the Father to fix / it —
He will blow-it. He fails
          and kills
His sons — and / *you* / know it.

Sylvia Plath

NICK AND
THE CANDLESTICK

I am a miner. The light burns blue.
Waxy stalactites
Drip and thicken, tears

The earthen womb
Exudes from its dead boredom.
Black bat airs

Wrap me, raggy shawls,
Cold homicides.
They weld to me like plums.

Old cave of calcium
Icicles, old echoer.
Even the newts are white,

Those holy Joes.
And the fish, the fish —
Christ! They are panes of ice,

A vice of knives,
A piranha
Religion, drinking

Its first communion out of my live toes.
The candle
Gulps and recovers its small altitude,

Its yellows hearten.
O love, how did you get here?
O embryo

Remembering, even in sleep,
Your crossed position.
The blood blooms clean

In you, ruby.
The pain
You wake to is not yours.

Love, love,
I have hung our cave with roses.
With soft rugs —

The last of Victoriana.
Let the stars
Plummet to their dark address,

Let the mercuric
Atoms that cripple drip
Into the terrible well,

You are the one
Solid the spaces lean on, envious.
You are the baby in the barn.

WHITE CENTER

Town or poem, I don't care how it looks. Old woman
take my hand and we'll walk one more time these streets
I believed marked me weak beneath catcalling clouds.
Long ago, the swamp behind the single row of stores
was filled and seeded. Roses today where Toughy Hassin
slapped my face to the grinning delight of his gang.
I didn't cry or run. Had I fought him
I'd have been beaten and come home bloody in tears
and you'd have told me I shouldn't be fighting.

Wasn't it all degrading, mean Mr. Kyte sweeping
the streets for no pay, believing what he'd learned
as a boy in England: "This is your community"?
I taunted him to rage, then ran. Is this the day
we call bad mothers out of the taverns and point them
sobbing for home, or issue costumes to posturing clowns
in the streets, make fun of drunk barbers, and hope
someone who left and made it returns, vowed
to buy more neon and give these people some class?

The Dugans aren't worth a dime, dirty Irish, nor days
you offered a penny for every fly I killed.
You were blind to my cheating. I saw my future certain —
that drunk who lived across the street and fell
in our garden reaching for the hoe you dropped.
All he got was our laughter. I helped him often home
when you weren't looking. I loved some terrible way
he lived in his mind and tried to be decent to others.
I loved the way we loved him behind our disdain.

Clouds. What glorious floating. They always move on
like I should have early. But your odd love and a war
taught me the world's gone evil past the first check point
and that's First Avenue South. I fell asleep each night
safe in love with my murder. The neighbor girl
plotted to tease every tomorrow and watch me turn
again to the woods and games too young for my age.
We never could account for the python cousin Warren
found half starved in the basement of Safeway.

It all comes back but in bites. I am the man
you beat to perversion. That was the drugstore MacCameron
flipped out in early one morning, waltzing
on his soda fountain. The siren married his shrieking.
His wife said, "We'll try again, in Des Moines."
You drove a better man into himself where he found tunes
he had no need to share. It's all beginning to blur
as it forms. Men cracking up or retreating.
Resolute women deep in hard prayer.

And it isn't the same this time. I hoped forty years
I'd write and would not write this poem. This town would die
and your grave never reopen. Or mine. Because I'm married
and happy, and across the street a foster child
from a cruel past is safe and need no longer crawl
for his meals, I walk this past with you, ghost in any field
of good crops, certain I remember everything wrong.
If not, why is this road lined thick with fern
and why do I feel no shame kicking the loose gravel home?

Linda Pastan

LETTER TO A SON
AT EXAM TIME

May again
and poems leaf out
from this old typewriter
shading the desk in half-light.
You at a college desk study different poems,
hold them warily by their dry stems —
so many leaves pressed to death
in a heavy book.

When you forget again
to call
it's poet and parent both
that you deny.
This is what I didn't know
I knew.

You woke up
on the wrong side
of my life.
For years I counted myself to sleep
on all the ways I might lose you:
death in its many-colored coat lounged
at the schoolhouse door, delivered
the milk, drove the carpool.

Now I catalogue leaves instead
on a weeping cherry.
It doesn't really weep,
nor do poets cry, so amazed
they are at the prosody
of pain.

You have a way with words yourself
you never asked for.
Though you disguise them
as best you can
in Gothic misspellings
there they stand in all their new muscle.
You will use them against me perhaps,
but you will use them.

Audre Lorde

A CHILD
SHALL LEAD

I have a child
whose feet are blind
on every road
but silence.

My boy has
lovely foolish lips
but cannot find
his way to sun

And I am grown
past knowledge.

Mark Strand

POT ROAST

I gaze upon the roast,
that is sliced and laid out
on my plate
and over it
I spoon the juices
of carrot and onion.
And for once I do not regret
the passage of time.

I sit by a window
that looks
on the soot-stained brick of buildings
and do not care that I see
no living thing — not a bird,
not a branch in bloom,
not a soul moving
in the rooms
behind the dark panes.
These days when there is little
to love or to praise
one could do worse
than yield
to the power of food.
So I bend

to inhale
the steam that rises
from my plate, and I think

of the first time
I tasted a roast
like this.
It was years ago
in Seabright,
Nova Scotia;
my mother leaned
over my dish and filled it
and when I finished
filled it again.
I remember the gravy,
its odor of garlic and celery,
and sopping it up
with pieces of bread.

And now
I taste it again.
The meat of memory.
The meat of no change.
I raise my fork
and I eat.

THE HAVING TO LOVE
SOMETHING ELSE

There was a man who would marry his mother, and asked his father for his mother's hand in marriage, and was told he could not marry his mother's hand because it was attached to all the rest of mother, which was all married to his father; that he'd have to love something else. . . .

And so he went into the world to love something else, and fell in love with a dining room.

He asked someone standing there, may I have this dining room's hand in marriage?

You may not, its hand is attached to all the rest of it, which has all been promised to me in connubial alliance, said someone standing there.

Just because the dining room lives in your house doesn't necessarily give you claim to its affections. . . .

Yes it does, for a dining room is always to be married to the heir apparent in the line of succession; after father it's my turn; and only if all mankind were destroyed could you succeed any other to the hand of this dining room. You'll have to love something else. . . .

And so the man who would marry his mother was again in the world looking for something to love that was not already loved. . . .

Lucille Clifton

THE LOST BABY POEM

the time i dropped your almost body down
down to meet the waters under the city
and run one with the sewage to the sea
what did i know about waters rushing back
what did i know about drowning
or being drowned

you would have been born into winter
in the year of the disconnected gas
and no car   we would have made the thin
walk over Genesee hill into the Canada wind
to watch you slip like ice into strangers' hands
you would have fallen naked as snow in winter
if you were here i could tell you these
and some other things

if i am ever less than a mountain
for your definite brothers and sisters
let the rivers pour over my head
let the sea take me for a spiller
of seas   let black men call me stranger
always   for your never named sake

MY MOTHER'S LIPS

Until I asked her to please stop doing it and was astonished to
     find that she not only could
but from the moment I asked her in fact would stop doing it,
     my mother, all through my childhood,
when I was saying something to her, something important,
     would move her lips as I was speaking
so that she seemed to be saying under her breath the very
     words I was saying as I was saying them.

Or, even more disconcertingly — wildly so now that my
     puberty had erupted — *before* I said them.
When I was smaller, I must just have assumed that she was
     omniscient. Why not?
She knew everything else — when I was tired, or lying; she'd
     know I was ill before I did.
I may even have thought — how could it not have come into
     my mind? — that she *caused* what I said.

All she was really doing of course was mouthing my words a
     split second after I said them myself,
but it wasn't until my own children were learning to talk that I
     really understood how,
and understood, too, the edge of anxiety in it, the wanting to
     bring you along out of the silence,
the compulsion to lift you again from those blank caverns of
     namelessness we encase.

That was long afterward, though: where I was now was just
     wanting to get her to stop,

and, considering how I brooded and raged in those days, how
  quickly my teeth went on edge,
the restraint I approached her with seems remarkable,
  although her so unprotestingly,
readily taming a habit by then three children and a dozen years
  old was as much so.

It's endearing to watch us again in that long-ago dusk, facing
  each other, my mother and me.
I've just grown to her height, or just past it: there are our lips
  moving together,
now the unison suddenly breaks, I have to go on by myself, no
  maestro, no score to follow.
I wonder what finally made me take umbrage enough, or heart
  enough, to confront her?

It's not important. My cocoon at that age was already
  unwinding: the threads ravel and snarl.
When I find one again, it's that two o'clock in the morning, a
  grim hotel on a square,
the impenetrable maze of an endless city, when, really alone
  for the first time in my life,
I found myself leaning from the window, incanting in a tearing
  whisper what I thought were poems.

I'd love to know what I raved that night to the night, what
  those innocent dithyrambs were,
or to feel what so ecstatically drew me out of myself and
  beyond . . . Nothing is there, though,
only the solemn piazza beneath me, the riot of dim, tiled roofs
  and impassable alleys,
my desolate bed behind me, and my voice, hoarse, and the
  sweet, alien air against me like a kiss.

THE LEAF PILE

Now here is a typical children's story
that happens in gorgeous October
when the mothers are coming
in the afternoon, wearing brisk boots
and windy skirts to pick up
the little children from the day care center

Frost in the air
the maples golden and crimson
my son in a leaf pile in the playground dreaming
I am late, the playground is almost
empty, my husband will kill me

I gather my son to go home,
he forgets his sweater in the playground and I send him back
he dawdles, he is playing with leaves
in his mind, it is already a quarter
to six, will you come on I say

and hurry along the corridor, there are yellow and blue rocket
paintings, but I feel bad and ask what did you do today,
do you recognize this story, the way he stands and picks
his nose, move I say, do you want dinner or not
I'm going to make a nice dinner, fried chicken

I wheedle, so could you please walk a little
faster, okay, I walk a little faster and get upstairs
myself, pivot on boot-heel, nobody there,

he is putting something in his mouth, his sable eyelashes
downcast, and I am swooping down the stairwell screaming

        damn you
        that's filthy
        I told you not before dinner

We are climbing the stairs
and I am crying, my son is not crying
I have shaken him, I have pried the sweet from his cheek
I have slapped his cheek like a woman slapping a carpet
with all my strength

        mothers are very strong
        he is too young to do anything about this
        will not remember he remembers it

The mind is a leaf pile where you can bury
anything, pain, the image of a woman
who wears a necklace of skulls, a screaming woman
you dig quickly and deposit the pulpy thing
you drop the leaves on it and it stays there, that is the story

that is sticking in my mind as we push
the exit door, and run through the evening wind
to my car where I jerk the gearshift and pick
up a little speed, going along
this neat suburban avenue full of maples
the mark of my hand a blush on my son's cheek.

Diane Wakoski

POEM FOR A LITTLE BOY
ON THE BUDDHA'S BIRTHDAY

You have
taken
a complete biography
in the form
of your mother's hand. Such a camera,
the lens
a blind measurer;
who cares
whether you will be president
if the coral scrapes
cuts the bottom of your feet as you walk
along the ocean floor,
who cares
where you are? Your mother never
forgets;
she does not however feel
the same salt.
                    Is there anything
                    more real
                    than imagination?

She does not even
know where you are.

Michael S. Harper

LECTURING ON THE
THEME OF MOTHERHOOD

The news is of camps, outpost, little progress;
I expect a bulletin from you on the latest
police foray into the projects, get it,
equal pay before the law, the only amendment
where angels talk to one another
about Friday, no eagles in evidence,
a few terns, almost broken apart in bottlecaps,
but who manage to fly.

Your grandson, Patrice, is playing basketball
in his football jersey; he says he can't cut
T's lawn because the place is ragged with daffodils —
his first recognition that flowers are the plateau
above the grave. He lies down in the gravel
driveway when asked to do chores, too close
to the free-throw line to shoot left-handed,
his natural delusion to your changing my grip
on a spoon at the highchair. I don't remember
the candy, told so often you're bound to forget
disappearance, the odor of shad Aunt Ede would make
after her trip to DeKalb Avenue, holding up traffic,
mind you, with a cane, which she rapped on the head-
lights of a bus, its white aura frolicking
in the police van driven by her students she knuckled
in the South Bronx, just before it burned down.

Michael S. Harper

MAMA'S REPORT

"Don't fight, honey,
don't let 'em catch you."

Tour over, gear packed,
hospital over, no job.

"Aw man, nothin' happened,"
explorer, altar boy —

Maybe it's 'cause they killed people
and don't know why they did?

My boy had color slides of dead people,
stacks of dead Vietnamese.

MP's asked if he'd been arrested
since discharge, what he'd been doin':

"Lookin' at slides,
lookin' at stacks of slides, mostly."

Fifteen minutes later a colonel called
from the Defense Department, said he'd won
                              the medal;

could he be in Washington with his family,
maybe he'd get a job now; he qualified.

The Democrats had lost, the president said;
there were signs of movement in Paris:

Charles Simic

SPOONS WITH REALISTIC
DEAD FLIES ON THEM

I cause great many worries to my mother.
My body will run with the weeds some day.
My head will be carried by slaughterhouse ants,
The carnivorous, bloody-aproned ants.

That was never in any of your legends, O saints!
The years she spent working in a novelty store:
Joy buzzers, false beards and dead flies
To talk to between the infrequent customers.

A room rented from a minor demon.
An empty bird cage and a coffee mill for company.
A hand-operated one for her secret guardian angel
To take a turn grinding the slow hours.

Though I'm not a believer —
Neither is she, and that's why she worries,
Looks both ways crossing the street
At two gusts of nothing and nothing.

Stephen Dunn

THE ROUTINE THINGS
AROUND THE HOUSE

When mother died
I thought: now I'll have a death poem.
That was unforgivable

yet I've since forgiven myself
as sons are able to do
who've been loved by their mothers.

I stared into the coffin
knowing how long she'd live,
how many lifetimes there are

in the sweet revisions of memory.
It's hard to know exactly
how we ease ourselves back from sadness,

but I remembered when I was twelve,
1951, before the world
unbuttoned its blouse.

I had asked my mother (I was trembling)
if I could see her breasts
and she took me into her room

without embarrassment or coyness
and I stared at them,
afraid to ask for more.

Now, years later, someone tells me
Cancers who've never had mother love
are doomed and I, a Cancer,

feel blessed again. What luck
to have had a mother
who showed me her breasts

when girls my age were developing
their separate countries,
what luck

she didn't doom me
with too much or too little.
Had I asked to touch,

perhaps to suck them,
what would she have done?
Mother, dead woman

who I think permits me
to love women easily,
this poem

is dedicated to where
we stopped, to the incompleteness
that was sufficient

and to how you buttoned up,
began doing the routine things
around the house.

Stanley Plumly

MY MOTHER'S FEET

How no shoe fit them,
and how she used to prop them,
having dressed for bed,
letting the fire in the coal-stove blue

and blink out, falling asleep in her chair.
How she bathed and dried them, night after night,
and rubbed their soreness like an intimacy.
How she let the fire pull her soft body through them.

She was the girl who grew just standing,
the one the picture cut at the knees.
She was the girl who seemed to be dancing
out on the lawn, after supper, alone.

I have watched her climb the militant stairs
and down again, watched the ground go out from under her.
I have seen her on the edge of chances —
she fell, when she fell, like a girl.

Someone who loved her said she walked on water.
Where there is no path nor wake. As a child
I would rise in the half-dark of the house,
from a bad dream or a noisy window,

something, almost, like snow in the air,
and wander until I could find those feet, propped
and warm as a bricklayer's hands,
every step of the way shining out of them.

EATING BABIES

1

Fat
is the soul of this flesh.
Eat with your hands, slow, you will understand
breasts, why everyone
adores them — Rubens' great custard nudes — why
we can't help sleeping with
pillows.

The old woman in the park pointed,
Is it yours?
Her gold eye-teeth gleamed.

I bend down, taste the fluted
nipples, the elbows, the pads
of the feet. Nibble earlobes, dip
my tongue in the salt fold
of shoulder and throat.

Even now he is changing
as if I were
licking him thin.

2

He squeezes his eyes tight
to hide
and blink! he's still here.
It's always a surprise.

Safety-fat,
angel-fat,

steal it in mouthfuls,
store it away
where you save
the face that you touched
for the last time
over and over,
your eyes closed

so it wouldn't go away.

3

Watch him sleeping. Touch
the pulse where
the bones haven't locked
in his damp hair:
the navel of dreams.
His eyes open for a moment, underwater.

His arms drift in the dark
as your breath
washes over him.

Bite one cheek. Again.
It's your own
life you lean over, greedy,
going back for more.

A NOTE ON
MY SON'S FACE

I

Tonight, I look, thunderstruck
at the gold head of my grandchild.
Almost asleep, he buries his feet
between my thighs;
his little straw eyes
close in the near dark.
I smell the warmth of his raw
slightly foul breath, the new death
waiting to rot inside him.
Our breaths equalize our heartbeats;
every muscle of the chest uncoils,
the arm bones loosen in the nest
of nerves. I think of the peace
of walking through the house,
pointing to the name of this, the name of that,
an educator of a new man.

Mother. Grandmother. Wise
Snake-woman who will show the way;
Spider-woman whose black tentacles
hold him precious. Or will tear off his head,
her teeth over the little husband,
the small fist clotted in trust at her breast.

This morning, looking at the face of his father,
I remembered how, an infant, his face was too dark,
nose too broad, mouth too wide.
I did not look in that mirror
and see the face that could save me
from my own darkness.
Did he, looking in my eye, see
what I turned from:
my own dark grandmother
bending over gladioli in the field,
her shaking black hand defenseless
at the shining cock of flower?

I wanted that face to die,
to be reborn in the face of a white child.

I wanted the soul to stay the same,
for I loved to death,
to damnation and God-death,
the soul that broke out of me.
I crowed: My Son! My Beautiful!
But when I peeked in the basket,
I saw the face of a black man.

Did I bend over his nose
and straighten it with my fingers
like a vine growing the wrong way?
Did he feel my hand in malice?

Generations we prayed and fucked
for this light child,
the shining god of the second coming;
we bow down in shame

and carry the children of the past
in our wallets, begging forgiveness.

I I

A picture in a book,
a lynching.
The bland faces of men who watch
a Christ go up in flames, smiling,
as if he were a hooked
fish, a felled antelope, some
wild thing tied to boards and burned.
His charring body
gives off light — a halo
burns out of him.
His face scorched featureless;
the hair matted to the scalp
like feathers.
One man stands with his hand on his hip,
another with his arm
slung over the shoulder of a friend,
as if this moment were large enough
to hold affection.

I I I

How can we wake
from a dream
we are born into,
that shines around us,
the terrible bright air?

Having awakened,
having seen our own bloody hands,
how can we ask forgiveness,

bring before our children the real
monster of their nightmare?

The worst is true.
Everything you did not want to know.

Bob Dylan

IT'S ALRIGHT, MA
(I'M ONLY BLEEDING)

Darkness at the break of noon
Shadows even the silver spoon
The handmade blade, the child's balloon
Eclipses both the sun and moon
To understand you know too soon
There is no sense in trying.

Pointed threats, they bluff with scorn
Suicide remarks are torn
From the fool's gold mouthpiece
The hollow horn plays wasted words
Proves to warn
That he not busy being born
Is busy dying.

Temptation's page flies out the door
You follow, find yourself at war
Watch waterfalls of pity roar
You feel to moan but unlike before
You discover
That you'd just be
One more person crying.

So don't fear if you hear
A foreign sound to your ear
It's alright, Ma, I'm only sighing.

As some warn victory, some downfall
Private reasons great or small
Can be seen in the eyes of those that call
To make all that should be killed to crawl
While others say don't hate nothing at all
Except hatred.

Disillusioned words like bullets bark
As human gods aim for their mark
Made everything from toy guns that spark
To flesh-colored Christs that glow in the dark
It's easy to see without looking too far
That not much
Is really sacred.

While preachers preach of evil fates
Teachers teach that knowledge waits
Can lead to hundred-dollar plates
Goodness hides behind its gates
But even the president of the United States
Sometimes must have
To stand naked.

An' though the rules of the road have been lodged
It's only people's games that you got to dodge
And it's alright, Ma, I can make it.

Advertising signs that con you
Into thinking you're the one
That can do what's never been done
That can win what's never been won
Meantime life outside goes on
All around you.

You lose yourself, you reappear
You suddenly find you got nothing to fear
Alone you stand with nobody near
When a trembling distant voice, unclear
Startles your sleeping ears to hear
That somebody thinks
They really found you.

A question in your nerves is lit
Yet you know there is no answer fit to satisfy
Insure you not to quit
To keep it in your mind and not fergit
That it is not he or she or them or it
That you belong to.

Although the masters make the rules
For the wise men and the fools
I got nothing, Ma, to live up to.

For them that must obey authority
That they do not respect in any degree
Who despise their jobs, their destinies
Speak jealously of them that are free
Cultivate their flowers to be
Nothing more than something
They invest in.

While some on principles baptized
To strict party platform ties
Social clubs in drag disguise
Outsiders they can freely criticize
Tell nothing except who to idolize
And then say God bless him.

While one who sings with his tongue on fire
Gargles in the rat race choir
Bent out of shape from society's pliers
Cares not to come up any higher
But rather get you down in the hole
That he's in.

But I mean no harm nor put fault
On anyone that lives in a vault
But it's alright, Ma, if I can't please him.

Old lady judges watch people in pairs
Limited in sex, they dare
To push fake morals, insult and stare
While money doesn't talk, it swears
Obscenity, who really cares
Propaganda, all is phony.

While them that defend what they cannot see
With a killer's pride, security
It blows the minds most bitterly
For them that think death's honesty
Won't fall upon them naturally
Life sometimes
Must get lonely.

My eyes collide head-on with stuffed graveyards
False gods, I scuff
At pettiness which plays so rough
Walk upside-down inside handcuffs
Kick my legs to crash it off
Say okay, I have had enough
What else can you show me?

And if my thought-dreams could be seen
They'd probably put my head in a guillotine
But it's alright, Ma, it's life, and life only.

Sharon Olds

RITES OF PASSAGE

As the guests arrive at my son's party
they gather in the living room —
short men, men in first grade
with smooth jaws and chins.
Hands in pockets, they stand around
jostling, jockeying for place, small fights
breaking out and calming. One says to another
How old are you? Six. I'm seven. So?
They eye each other, seeing themselves
tiny in the other's pupils. They clear their
throats a lot, a room of small bankers,
they fold their arms and frown. *I could beat you
up*, a seven says to a six,
the dark cake, round and heavy as a
turret, behind them on the table. My son,
freckles like specks of nutmeg on his cheeks,
chest narrow as the balsa keel of a
model boat, long hands
cool and thin as the day they guided him
out of me, speaks up as a host
for the sake of the group.
We could easily kill a two-year-old,
he says in his clear voice. The other
men agree, they clear their throats
like Generals, they relax and get down to
playing war, celebrating my son's life.

Sharon Olds

THE LATEST INJURY

When my son comes home from the weekend trip where he
stood up into a piece of steel in the
ceiling of a car and cut open his head and
had the wound shaved and sprayed
and stitches taken, he comes up to me
grinning with pride and fear and slowly
bows his head, as if to the god of trauma,
and there it is, his scalp blue-grey as the
skin of a corpse, the surface cold and
gelatinous, the long split
straight as if deliberate, the
sutures on either side like terrible
marks of human will. I say
Amazing, I press his head to my stomach
gently, the naked skin on top
quivering like the skin on boiled milk and
bluish as the epidermis of a monkey
drawn out of his mother dead, the
faint growth of fine hair like a
promise. I rock his brain in my arms as I
once rocked his whole body,
delivered, and the wound area glows
grey and translucent as a fledgling's head when it
teeters on the edge of the nest, the cut a
midline down the skull, the flesh
jelly, the stitches black, the slit saying
taken, the thread saying given back.

James Tate

FOR MOTHER
ON FATHER'S DAY

You never got to recline
in the maternal tradition,
I never let you. Fate,

you call it, had other eyes,
for neither of us ever had
a counterpart in the way

familial traditions go.
I was your brother,
and you were my unhappy

neighbor. I pitied you
the way a mother pities
her son's failure. I could

never find the proper
approach. I would have
lent you sugar, mother.

DISTANCE FROM LOVED ONES

After her husband died, Zita decided to get the face-lift she had
always wanted. Halfway through the operation her blood
pressure started to drop, and they had to stop. When Zita
tried to fasten her seat belt for her sad drive home, she threw
out her shoulder. Back at the hospital the doctor examined
her and found cancer run rampant throughout her shoulder
and arm and elsewhere. Radiation followed. And, now, Zita
just sits there in her beauty parlor, bald, crying and crying.
My mother tells me all this on the phone, and I say: Mother, who
is Zita?
And my mother says, I am Zita. All my life I have been Zita, bald
and crying. And you, my son, who should have known me
best, thought I was nothing but your mother.
But, Mother, I say, I am dying. . . .

Louise Gluck

THE GIFT

Lord, You may not recognize me
speaking for someone else.
I have a son. He is
so little, so ignorant.
He likes to stand
at the screen door, calling
oggie, oggie, entering
language, and sometimes
a dog will stop and come up
the walk, perhaps
accidentally. May he believe
this is not an accident?
At the screen
welcoming each beast
in love's name, Your emissary.

NIGHT PIECE

He knows he will be hurt.
The warnings come to him in bed
because repose threatens him: in the camouflaging
light of the nightlight, he pretends to guard
the flesh in which his life is summarized.
He spreads his arms. On the wall, a corresponding figure
links him to the darkness he cannot control.
In its forms, the beasts originate
who are his enemies. He cannot sleep
apart from them.

Tess Gallagher

EACH BIRD WALKING

Not while, but long after he had told me,
I thought of him, washing his mother, his
bending over the bed and taking back
the covers. There was a basin of water
and he dipped a washrag in and
out of the basin, the rag
dripping a little onto the sheet as he
turned from the bedside to the nightstand
and back, there being no place

on her body he shouldn't touch because
he had to and she helped him, moving
the little she could, lifting so he could
wipe under her arms, a dipping motion
in the hollow. Then working up from
the feet, around the ankles, over the
knees. And this last, opening
her thighs and running the rag firmly
and with the cleaning thought
up through her crotch, between the lips,
over the V of thin hairs —

as though he were a mother
who had the excuse of cleaning to touch
with love and indifference
the secret parts of her child, to graze
the sleepy sexlessness in its waiting
to find out what to do for the sake

of the body, for the sake of what only
the body can do for itself.

So his hand, softly at the place
of his birth-light. And she, eyes deepened
and closed in the dim room.
And because he told me her death as
important to his being with her,
I could love him another way. Not
of the body alone, or of its making,
but carried in the white spires of trembling
until what spirit, what breath we were
was shaken from us. Small then,
the word *holy*.
He turned her on her stomach
and washed the blades of her shoulders, the
small of her back. "That's good," she said,
"that's enough."

On our lips that morning, the tart juice
of the mothers, so strong in remembrance, no
asking, no giving, and what you said, this
being the end of our loving, so as not to hurt
the closer one to you, made me look
to see what was left of us
with our sex taken away. "Tell me," I said,
"something I can't forget." Then the story of
your mother, and when you finished
I said, "That's good, that's enough."

Rodney Jones

CAUGHT

There is in the human voice
A quavery vowel sometimes,
More animal than meaning,
More mineral than gentle,

A slight nuance by which my
Mother would recognize lies,
Detect scorn or envy, sober
Things words would not admit,

Though it's true the best liars
Must never know they lie.
They move among good-byes
Worded like congratulations

We listen for and hear until
Some misery draws us back
To what it really was they
Obviously meant not to say.

And misery often draws us
Out to meadows or trees,
That speechless life where
Everything inhuman is true.

Mother spoke for tentative
People, illiterate, unsure.
Thinking of it her way is to
Reduce all words to tones

The wind might make anytime
With a few dead leaves. Our
Own names called in the dark
Or quail rising. Sounds that

Go straight from the ear to
The heart. There all the time,
They are a surface too clear
To see. Written down, no

Matter how right, they are too
Slow and vain as those soft
Vows we spoke in childhood to
Wild things, birds or rabbits

We meant to charm. When
My mother mentioned oaks,
They could be cut down, sawn
Into boards and nailed together

As rooms, and she was mostly
Quiet, standing in the kitchen,
Her pin rolling like law
Across plains of biscuit dough

While dark ripened, wind
Died on the tongue of each leaf.
The night broke in pieces
If she cleared her throat.

THE BAD MOTHER

Remember that in the evening, just at supper
we would sometimes see
children burning.

You were just a baby.
I would rock you in front of the TV
your father would come home late
from his work, and sometimes
not for days.

I would rock you there and
each time they showed the dead people
or a young boy screaming
I would stiffen and you would start to cry.

Then later, when we were alone, all the time,
the walls would collapse
around me and I would have gone myself
straight into the picture and stood
with the others.
You crying in the evening had become
a pattern of living.

I was the good mother.

The bad mother left her children behind
and was on television
becoming a fanatic,

crazy: she spent two years
in prison, not eating,
while her children were home, alone, waiting
for their mother, the bad mother.

They kept
a Christmas tree standing for two years
until she came back.

AN EARLY DEATH

It is the first death that seems so open
   to revision, as if later on,
      at some ordinary hour, the dead
         will again be with us wherever we are.

It was a Catholic funeral for the boy
   who came home one day, went to sleep
      in the lasting light of early summer,
         and didn't wake up for the evening meal.

During the service I watched his mother,
   who was Spanish, as the event burned
      dimly in her, the off-red of roses
         almost dry, a small pulsing emanation,

not light exactly but something just barely
   aglow. They couldn't agree on the cause
      of death, but for me he was just gone,
         first one day and then all the others.

It occurs to me these many years later
   that the funeral provided me
      an introduction, and then the possibility
         of resuming my own life, although

I often thought I saw my friend trimming
   the ivy in front of his house on Chandler
      during the endless summer afternoons
         of the San Fernando Valley,

the silver cross he wore filmed with dirt
        kicked up by the trimmer. By autumn
            I was able to let him go.
                He no longer appeared on our street

in his white parochial-school shirts.
        Sometimes, when I sat with his mother
            while she prepared her survivor's meal
                and we talked in a casual way

of her son, I studied the large reproduction
        of Velázquez's *Surrender of Breda*
            that hung on a wall near the kitchen
                where we sat. I counted the horses

and soldiers as they stood in a line,
        their spears held upright, catching a diminished
            amber light, posing as if for Velázquez
                himself, impatient to remove their armor

and return to the tables of Rioja
        and heavy bread. It is the quality
            of light in that painting that brings back
                my friend's Spanish mother, the vermilion

smoldering like old fire behind
        the horsemen, under the unilluminated
            green shake of the deciduous trees
                Velázquez chose to leave out of the painting.

She talked quietly about her son
        as she prepared her meals. Her sorrow
            was alive, unrelinquished, without
                revision. She often tried to explain

how he cared for me, our friendship;
the vocabulary was hers, her meaning
embarrassing information at that age.
She allowed me to return

something of her son, although this certainly
didn't occur to me then, and perhaps
not for many years.
It is afternoon on the East Coast —

when I think of my friend
it is she who is there, who takes his place.
We have both lived out that early death,
and we have this far survived the austere light

that fixes those men in *Surrender*
of Breda, each of them waiting around
under the protection of Velázquez's
invisible trees, in the little light left them.

Anne Waldman

COMPLAYNT

after Emily Dickinson

I'm wanton — no I've stopped that,
That old place
I've changed, I'm Mother
It's more mysterious.
How odd the past looks
When I reread old notebooks,
See their faces fade
I feel it everywhere
& ordinary too
Am I safer now?
Was other way gayer?
I'm Mother now, O help &
Continue!

Philip Schultz

FOR MY MOTHER

The hand of peace you sent from Israel
hangs on my wall like an ironic testament
to the one quality we have never shared.
I imagine you peering into that ancient vista
as if discovering God in the brilliant sunlight,
worrying no doubt about your bunions & weak ankles.
These words have been a long time in coming.
Once I wrote only to the dead but grief has an end.
The living are more demanding. I have seen the scar
big as a zipper on your belly where they cut you open
& ripped out six pounds of hunger demanding to be adored.
You named me Big Mouth, Big Pain, Big Wanting. Sons,
you said, suck a woman dry & leave for someone
with stronger ankles & a back better suited
to their talent for self-eulogy. Yes, men
are more selfish. Nothing demands of us
so absolute a generosity. But I have given up
the umbilicus of rage which for so long has fed me.
Now I understand why you paste every scrap of my existence
in a black book like a certificate of blood, but achievement
is not redemption & even now I cannot hold a woman
without fearing she might take too much of me. Perhaps
this is why I love a woman most during her time
when the earth is lush within her & her embrace
gives forth such privilege my passion for distance
becomes a cry for forgiveness, a desire to return
always to the beginning. No, I have not forgotten
the Saturday afternoons in movie houses when you
cried so softly I imagined I was to blame.

I remember those long walks home,
our hands a binding of such unbreakable vengeance
I can still taste the cool blue wafers of your eyes.
Believe me, there was nothing I would not have given,
nothing I would not have done for you. Remember our game
when I held your leg so tightly you had to drag me
like a ball & chain around our unhappy house? Neither of us
understood that the grip of consanguinity is nothing less
than an embrace with time. Mother, though I cannot unhinge
all this lasting sorrow or make your flesh sing, cannot
return the gift of such remarkable expansion, I am always
thinking: This is for you, this word, this breath, this tiny light,
this, my hand of peace, this wound which does not heal.

Joan Murray

MADONNA VS. CHILD

for my son Jim

I

I expect no man to understand.
The womb has so complicated everything.
        Someday in a business suit
you may stop at lunchtime and
      picture yourself tucked up in
the broody gloom of the ovary and stirred one night
by a quick ejaculation.
      It's embarrassing. At best, confusing.
More comfortable, a conception in a glass
or stainless steel, sanitized and
sealed, no cleaving bonds.
              But flesh will not forget its
groaning, momentary, pinioned breach of
freedom as you came,
    your greasy, bloody head intruding
in the mirror where there had been nothing.
And the moment extends itself:
              forever pinioned
beneath a thing that emerged
raw and weighty as a batch of clay, and
    trailing that leeching cord.
How ugly we both were, battered and exhausted
as something forced us into those complicated
              and absurd postures
and insisted that all this be done.
I expect no man will fully understand.

I won't ask more of you.
None of this was my design. I
would have been glad to find you dropped among
the split wood of the fireplace
and hear the wings rushing away,
the voiceless clatter of the unburdened bird
                    drifting through the downdraft.

   I I

And now the balance is undone,
    the calm keel jostled by your coming.
Our wills wrestle above the crib, and you,
squat stowaway, must win.
Overpowering with frailty, your
                            trivial fingers flare out
their distress, your lungs raise up
a tyrant SOS.
Once I could have stood aloof
    like a watcher on some isolated shore, amused at
the excesses of a courting sandpiper's
                            ruffled-up display.
But your long conspiracy with nature is too shrewd:
I am at your will.
I offer my breast to you, as I would to no other
                            stranger.
You
    will survive.
Take your place before me in this boat where
I once sat, assured of my own skin.
Your weight pitches the balance I had managed to maintain.
      In the end, I know it is I
who must go over.

III

How easy it will be to say this
　　　　　once it's said.
It will pale the pinks and blues of nurseries,
the maternity gowns with their flowery collars, hanging
　　　in the attics, the paper cards with everyone's
　　　　　　congratulations, bundled up in rubber bands.
Look instead at the ties which we must
wear forever now, clownish
as a pair of actors dressed
　　　　　in schoolboy clothes, for the bond still holds us
to who we were on that erupting morning,
　　　and fixes us, madonna and child, by the flesh.
Look at our other postures, each one contrived
dissoluble, changing daily, hourly:
a head bowed in disappointment, a shoulder
slouched in disregard, a finger flying out with
　　　　　accusation, a foot drumming
　　　　　　　　　　its impatience.
Each pose collapses
beneath the weight of our anatomy:
　　　　　　　　　of where you began
before you became.
If you think that imposes too much on you,
understand it is impossible for either one of
　　　us to wriggle free.
Child, you are my future. I am your history.

Minnie Bruce Pratt

POEM FOR MY SONS

When you were born, all the poets I knew
were men, dads eloquent on their sleeping
babes and the future: Coleridge at midnight,
Yeats' prayer that his daughter lack opinions,
his son be high and mighty, think and act.
You've read the new father's loud eloquence,
fiery sparks written in a silent house
breathing with the mother's exhausted sleep.

When you were born, my first, what I thought was
milk: my breasts sore, engorged, but not enough
when you woke.   With you, my youngest, I did not
think: my head unraised for three days, mind-dead
from waist-down anesthetic labor, saddle
block, no walking either.
                                        Your father was then
the poet I'd ceased to be when I got married.
It's taken me years to write this to you.

I had to make a future, willful, voluble,
lascivious, a thinker, a long walker,
unstruck transgressor, furious, shouting,
voluptuous, a lover, a smeller of blood,
milk, a woman mean as she can be some nights,
existence I could pray to, capable of
poetry.
              Now here we are.   You are men,
and I am not the woman who rocked you
in the sweet reek of penicillin, sour milk,

the girl who could not imagine herself
or a future more than a warm walled room,
had no words but the pap of the expected,
and so, those nights, could not wish for you.

But now I have spoken, my self, I can ask
for you: that you'll know evil when you smell it;
that you'll know good and do it, and see how both
run loose through your lives; that then you'll remember
you come from dirt and history; that you'll choose
memory, not anesthesia; that you'll have work
you love, hindering no one, a path crossing
at boundary markers where you question power;
that your loves will match you thought for thought
in the long heat of blood and fact of bone.

Words not so romantic nor so grandly tossed
as if I'd summoned the universe to be
at your disposal.
                    I can only pray:

That you'll never ask for the weather, earth,
angels, women, or other lives to obey you;

that you'll remember me, who crossed, recrossed
you,
            as a woman making slowly toward
an unknown place where you could be with me,
like a woman on foot, in a long stepping out.

A WAVING HAND

Last night of the visit, the youngest put his head
down, saying, *Again and again and again and again
and again*, his head down on the bed.
                                        I said
we should get a medal for every time we say good-bye,
like a purple heart; or we could have a waving hand
(*Like the one in the windows of roaring trucks*,
he says).
            Our chests would be heavy with
medals, heavy waving hands: pendulum:

we come back, we say hello.   He cheered up, then.

Yusef Komunyakaa

VENUS'S-FLYTRAPS

I am five,
   Wading out into the deep
     Sunny grass,
Unmindful of snakes
   & yellowjackets, out
     To the yellow flowers
Quivering in sluggish heat.
   Don't mess with me
     'Cause I have my Lone Ranger
Six-shooter. I can hurt
   You with questions
     Like silver bullets.
The tall flowers in my dreams are
   Big as the First State Bank,
     & they eat all the people
Except the ones I love.
   They have women's names,
     With mouths like where
Babies come from. I am five.
   I'll dance for you
     If you close your eyes. No
Peeping through your fingers.
   I don't supposed to be
     This close to the tracks.
One afternoon I saw
   What a train did to a cow.
     Sometimes I stand so close

I can see the eyes
   Of men hiding in boxcars.
      Sometimes they wave
& holler for me to get back. I laugh
   When trains make the dogs
      Howl. Their ears hurt.
I also know bees
   Can't live without flowers.
      I wonder why Daddy
Calls Mama honey.
   All the bees in the world
      Live in little white houses.
Except the ones in these flowers.
   All sticky & sweet inside.
      I wonder what death tastes like.
Sometimes I toss the butterflies
   Back into the air.
      I wish I knew why
The music in my head
   Makes me scared.
      But I know things
I don't supposed to know.
   I could start walking
      & never stop.
These yellow flowers
   Go on forever.
      Almost to Detroit.
Almost to the sea.
   My mama says I'm a mistake.
      That I made her a bad girl.
My playhouse is underneath
   Our house, & I hear people
      Telling each other secrets.

SEVEN MONTHS

A slight infection of the ear,
then plain cold human will:
his whole body said no.
He stiffened in her arms, screamed
to see the nipple bared.
After two days of pumped milk and tears,
screamed even at the great white bra
when she unbuttoned her blouse.
She tried singing, coaxed the baby
close, then as he fell to sleep,
tricked him with the gradual
transfer from bottle to body.
He shuddered, his lips moved
half-opened on her skin and he took back
the hard, veined breast
swollen as big as his head.
Pain was part of it; she ached
with relief as his clean taut pull
drew the arrows from her chest.
She settled back in the rocker —
dim pinpoints of stars, moths
tapping the screen. Ordinary September.
But the little mouth was resolute:
last time, last time
went the rhythm of its suck.
Why now, she cried, allowing
her voice to fill the still room,
then pulled herself in and sanely
gave him up.

Michael Burkard

A RAINCOAT

My mother kisses me goodnight for the thousandth time.
I am always wondering now, is this the last kiss?
Is this the end — for I have begun to see the face of the end
and it is not such a dark end, nor wholly white with light.
It is as if one will don a raincoat for a journey into eternity.
That is the most I can say about this face.
My mother's face — ahh! Now that I forgave myself I can see
    her face

and it is more beautiful now
than ever before in its seventy years.
And to think I worry about my face, and you
yours! How foolish.
My darling I told you my memory was forming in a central
    place
around a raincoat. And my young friend, whom I feuded with
as only friends will, walking to school with me in abject silence
(we were feuding but walking together!)

and my brother attempting to break the silence for us.
It broke, I know it broke, I don't know when and where
but yes it broke . . .

and did I tell you I might see death before any of us . . . and I
    say this
not to frighten us but to tell you it is alright, to tell myself
it is alright . . . it is believable

and death is so broke it needs us . . .
I believe the momentum of a life never, never stops . . .
the breath never ceases . . . the moon and the sycamore never
     cease to
miss us as we miss them . . .

A raincoat — I cannot even begin to articulate this coat . . .
the lives it saw, the leaves it saw orphaned at the school,
the words like orphans which fell against the silent night
from a child's mouth. The breath of the closet like a stone
     filled
with light as the closet knew the moon or sun rose . . .

the paint which married one of its sleeves . . .
the coy view the raincoat possessed of my mother and my
     sister . . .
if this raincoat could have met you darling . . .

people's faces . . . in the square, in the school, in the window
     our souls
climbed at night when we slept in each other's arms . . . the
     faces at sea
accompanying the faces on the roads to the sea . . . the faces
     of your
sons and your daughter, my mother and my father, the lost
     ones who
love us without our ever knowing . . . how constant they are

in this life and death which is one beauty . . .
Shh! A child is hanging his raincoat . . . my mother
kisses us goodnight . . .

THE MOTHER'S TALE

Once when I was young, Juanito,
there was a ballroom in Lima
where Hernán, your father,
danced with another woman
and I cut him across the cheek
with a pocketknife.
Oh, the pitch of the music sometimes,
the smoke and rustle of crinoline.
But what things to remember now
on your wedding day.
I pour a kettle of hot water
into the wooden tub where you are sitting.
I was young, free.
But Juanito, how free is a woman?—
born with Eve's sin between her legs,
and inside her,
Lucifer sits on a throne of abalone shells,
his staff with the head of John the Baptist
skewered on it.
And in judgment, son, in judgment he says
that women will bear the fruit of the tree
we wished so much to eat
and that fruit will devour us
generation by generation,

so my son,
you must beat Rosita often.
She must know the weight of a man's hand,
the bruises that are like the wounds of Christ.

Her blood that is black at the heart
must flow until it is as red and pure as His.
And she must be pregnant always
if not with child
then with the knowledge
that she is alive because of you.
That you can take her life
more easily than she creates it,
that suffering is her inheritance from you
and through you, from Christ,
who walked on his mother's body
to be the King of Heaven.

CHILDHOOD

How it is I returned
to this one memory all
morning and through mid-
afternoon could not work,
confused still by what
had, or would not, come
back to me: a few small
drops of rain on my
Sunday shoes, the sun
plunged into the rose-gray
summit behind the woods,
and settling, overhead,
like waterbirds (you can't
tell how many, their wings
overlapping), the high yellow
clouds, and a voice, at
intervals, calling my name
across that farflung
sky — no, across the disced
back pasture where I
had wandered, not lost or
frightened, but as in a drift
of leaves — and so it was
I turned then and saw, not you,
but a winter moon rising
out of the suburbs like a pearl
earring lifted into place
by a hand, too long ago,

to be sure, to know what
it means, or the time
it takes, which was all
your life, Mother, and
all of mine.

Mark Rudman

THE NOWHERE WATER

We ate alone in the immense dining room.
She got me to eat each night
by saying any meat was buffalo meat.
The desert had the silence of one who waits.
Cool water, clear water — she sang.
Her voice soothed my deepest blood
as I listened to her sing it over and over;
she knew just how to prolong

cool — clear — water — .
The desert was vast and empty.
Water nowhere, neither cool nor clear.
My one friend lived in a trailer in a dust bowl.
I'd wander off alone and once
got far enough away to where
the bleaching neon of the strip
dwindled to tinsel.

Everywhere we went men were after her.
One clear night we were walking home
hand in hand in the dark.
No moon, but the road was lit
by gas station globes
and not-too-distant hotels,
when a silver-haired man
behind the red wheel of

a white Caddy convertible
stalked alongside
and offered us a ride.
She gripped my hand; panic
coursed through us, our spines rigid.
"Don't look, just keep walking."
Soon she would be married again.
What a waste of beauty — and all on my account.

There is no love like the love
of sons for mothers.
And the seedy silver-haired man,
and his measured, robotic voice,
has hunted me since —
and enters me tonight
through The Talking Heads' searing,
apocalyptic version of the song. . . .

These were the best moments of my life,
alone in Vegas for six weeks
keeping a beautiful woman company
while she obtained her divorce.

Rachel Hadas

UP AND DOWN

Days into weeks.
Still night sweats
and bleeding still,
its bleachy smell.
Your bleat softly
shears the thick
fleece of dark.
I wake wet,
cold, hot:
milk and sweat,
nightgown, hair,
humid breasts.
Here you are.
Latch on.
Suck.

Lie down, says the old body.
Get back between the sheets.
Root down, down in dreams.

Your soft call cries no more alternatives.
The bed, the night
make space for three of us.
Silent accommodations in the dark.

Lawrence Joseph

MAMA REMEMBERS

I tried to do what I was told, made
the sign of the cross before icons
of the Apostles and my prayer equal
fat Father Riashi sweating, incanting

Syriac surrounded by incense smoke
in Our Lady of Redemption Melchite Church
my fifth Palm Sunday. Did I know
arteries hardened, the business

was changed by years of no money,
there was a miscarriage, in January,
on Thursday, in the kitchen, in 1951?
Grandpa, legless, appeared to me alone

in dazzling hot September afternoon.
Mama could not know how not to be sad.
In the sunroom before the picture window
Aunt Rose and Aunt Angele compared

the color of my skin to old Uncle Moise's.
There was enough silence to divide.
My brother did not tell what he knew,
took his share, whatever he could.

Did I believe grandma's eyes revealed
her will to live or her need to die?
Mama remembers if my father ever cried.
Mama remembers how much she cried.

Frank Stanford

TERRORISM

While my mother is washing the black socks
Of her religion,
I climb out of the washtub,
Stinking clean like the moon and the suds
In my ass,
The twenty she earned last week in my teeth,
My shoes and my pistol wrapped in my pants,
Slip off the back porch
And head down the road, buck naked and brave,
But lonely, because it's fifteen hours
By bus to the capital
And nobody will know
How it feels to nail down a heart
Black as tarpaper.
Mother, when you beat out my quilt tomorrow,
Remember the down in the sunlight,
Because I did not sleep there.
Remember, come evening, the last hatch of mayflies,
Because I won't.
They are evil, mother, and I am
Going to take it all out, in one motion,
The way you taught me to clean a fish,
Until all that is left is the memory of their voice,
And I will work that dark loose
From the backbone with my thumb.
Mother, the sad dance on fire.

Bruce Smith

AMERICAN LUNCH

Lebanon Bologna and meat loaf, two sandwiches
in wax paper and some carrot sticks
or celery in wax paper, milk, and a Tasty
Cake butterscotch krimpet, occasionally
a French apple pie or the same thing with salami
and cheese, but once a dark pomegranate, fall
so I'm playing football.
I sit down with my thick compatriots
and out it rolls.
        "You idiots,
you've never seen one of these?"
Blood red grenade, flesh slit, thumb stained, membranes
and seed inside of seeds inside a brown paper sack
that my mother packed
and I blew up and exploded.

Terese Svoboda

ON MY FIRST SON
after Ben Jonson

Goodbye, Deng, Spirit-of-the-Air,
my joy was motherlove to bear

his five years in hope and now in
grief as sweet as some great sin.

O that I could still catch and hold
him! He would do as he were told.

Not even science could reverse
a simple accident: the curse

of life that will not stick. I say:
here lies all reason for poetry,

for whose sake I promise to love no less
the next child who claims my happiness.

Kate Daniels

from *THE NIOBE POEMS*
LYING DOWN

Nothing moves
in the house. A huge
silence, tense and quivering
as the hand of the masseuse
cupped barely above the body,
heat pouring down
in gentle sheets, the fine hairs
flickering up, underneath.

There is a smell of many flowers,
a heaviness of many shoes
still caked with mud
from the open grave.
They are lying down now
in separate rooms.
The scenes in their heads
keep stalling:
They see the diver surfacing
with the dripping body.
They see him weeping, alone,
at the end of the dock.
They see the diver, the body,
the weeping, the dock.

There is a cry from a darkened room
as utterly undone
as the guttural sounds
of giving birth.
But Niobe never hurt
this much giving birth
and nothing has prepared her
for the size of this.
She sees herself as never before:
the love she thought
so pure to sin:
she wants other boys dead
and her boy back.

Niobe lying on the bed
is so ugly with love,
nothing like a mother:
disfigured, untender.
But god keeps going
at her. He opens
the door wider and bids them look.
He wants them to know
how hideous it is
where Niobe lives. How sentimental
and careless they've always been.
They've never seen anything
clearly. They've understood
nothing. He's god.
They're a bunch of dumb assholes.

Rika Lesser

WOMAN FROM CHIANCIANO*

My child won't stir,
stares up at me all
supplication. Arms
close to his sides, knees
bent, his tiny feet rest
on an arm of this
chair. Swaddled in cloth
not thick enough to
warm, perhaps he sleeps.
I neither sleep nor
move: I hold him on
my thighs, the weight of
his head on my strong
right arm, his body
in my two huge hands
that press firmly and
softly into his
formless back. My eyes
are open, fix on empty
space. They cannot see
his smile of trust. Still,
we are one, this knowledge
surges through the stone.

The arms of my throne,
twin watchdogs, sphinxes'
wings; thick hair

bound and crowned, their heads
press against my knees.
They gape — one in surprise,
the other in dismay.

They hold me here
unmoving as the folds
of cloth that fall
resolutely, cushion,
and hem me in.
                              Inside
I can feel some other
shape, older than my own:
A woman's head that once
served wine, now holds dust
and bones of a child
not yet born.

---

*She is a limestone cinerary statue, 0.9 meters high, from the territory of Chiusi, and
dates from ca. 450 B.C.; in the Museo Archeològico, Florence. Her head functions as a
lid. Found inside her, along with a gold fibula, was an Attic *oinochoe* in the shape of a
woman's head.

Cornelius Eady

MY MOTHER, IF SHE HAD WON
FREE DANCE LESSONS

Would she have been a person
With a completely different outlook on life?
There are times when I visit
And find her settled on a chair
In our dilapidated house,
The neighborhood crazy lady
Doing what the neighborhood crazy lady is supposed to do,
Which is absolutely nothing.

And I wonder as we talk our sympathetic talk,
Abandoned in easy dialogue,
I, the son of the crazy lady,
Who crosses easily into her point of view
As if yawning
Or taking off an overcoat.
Each time I visit
I walk back into our lives

And I wonder, like any child who wakes up one day to find
     themself
Abandoned in a world larger than their Bad dreams,
I wonder as I see my mother sitting there,
Landed to the right-hand window in the living room,
Pausing from time to time in the endless loop of our dialogue
To peek for rascals through the
Venetian blinds,

I wonder a small thought.
I walk back into our lives.
Given the opportunity,
How would she have danced?
Would it have been as easily
As we talk to each other now,
The crazy lady
And the crazy lady's son,
As if we were old friends from opposite coasts
Picking up the thread of a long conversation,

Or two ballroom dancers
Who only know
One step?

What would have changed
If the phone had rung like a suitor,
If the invitation had arrived in the mail
Like Jesus, extending a hand?

Louise Erdrich

SHELTER

My four adopted sons in photographs
wear solemn black. Their faces comprehend
their mother's death, an absence in a well
of empty noise, and Otto strange and lost.
Her name was Mary also, Mary Kröger.
Two of us have lived and one is gone.
Her hair was blond; it floated back in wings,
and still you see her traces in the boys:
bright hair and long, thin, knotted woman's hands.
I knew her, Mary Kröger, and we were bosom friends.
All graves are shelters for our mislaid twins.

Otto was for many years her husband,
and that's the way I always thought of him.
I nursed her when she sickened and the cure
fell through at Rochester. The healing bath
that dropped her temperature, I think, too fast.
I was in attendance at her death:
She sent the others out. She rose and gripped my arm
and tried to make me promise that I'd care
for Otto and the boys. I had to turn away
as my own mother had when her time came.
How few do not return in memory
and make us act in ways we can't explain.
I could not lie to ease her, living, dying.
All graves are full of such accumulation.
And yet, the boys were waiting in New York
to take the first boat back to Otto's folks
in Germany, prewar, dark powers were at work,

and Otto asked me on the westbound bus
to marry him. I could not tell him no —
We help our neighbors out. I loved him though

It took me several years to know I did
from that first time he walked in to deliver
winter food. Through Father Adler's kitchen,
he shouldered half an ox like it was bread
and looked at me too long for simple greeting.
This is how our lives complete themselves,
as effortless as weather, circles blaze
in ordinary days, and through our waking selves
they reach, to touch our true and sleeping speech.

So I took up with Otto, took the boys
and watched for them, and made their daily bread
from what the grocer gave them in exchange
for helping him. It's hard to tell you how
they soon became so precious I got sick
from worry, and woke up for two months straight
and had to check them, sleeping, in their beds,
and had to watch and see each breathe or move
before I could regain my sleep again.
All graves are pregnant with our nearest kin.

Martín Espada

THE SECRET OF THE
LEGAL SECRETARY'S
CIGARETTE SMOKE

for my mother

Cubicled women
pecking at computers,
observed by the senior partner
bowed and vigilant
as a gray monk,
watch in hand
at exactly 9 A.M.

Genuflection
to ashen priests of commerce,
bodies gliding in a hush
across the carpet
to leave coffee and pastries
for aristocratic hands
to contemplate.

At break time,
the senior partner's name
is a spat breath of cigarette smoke,
and even the quiet
religious woman
sneers.

Liz Rosenberg

THE POEM OF MY HEART

The milk-spray glitters along our newborn's cheek.
A power surge plunges us into darkness for half a second
and then I hoist him by his footed suit and lower him like a
    boom into his crib.
In this dim, Christmasy light, which we think is the lost light of
    stars,
the San Gabriel azaleas are opening their rose-pink petals as
    slowly as the mouths of women
about to say something wonderful.

Snow glitters on the new year, in a wave tossed over from the
    old.
Time, almost palpable, time twittering through the air
or gliding slowly down a pole into a crowd of tens of thousands
cheering — incredibly, cheering on — the passage of their lives;
blowing horns and wearing paper-cone hats, like children
at that ecstatic instant when the cake is served,
before it is eaten.

Tonight we walked our new son to a high-school parking lot
where we spend all our New Year's Eves —
we marched him lolling sleepy against his father's stomach
as last year this time, a multiplying seed he rode
inside of mine, learning the loop-the-loops of locomotion,
because I walked and rocked him all that spring, block after
    block,
walked miles, as if by constant motion I could slowly
pull him forward with me out into the world —
So he's learned to distrust stillness,

and as soon as we'd reached the parking lot,
and sat,
he woke and cried
and we stood up and walked him home again.

Welcome to the new year, you to whom everything is new!
The first flakes of a snowstorm stung like sea-foam in our faces,
turning the navy-blue sky murky
the way it does
that instant before it all dissolves
into the floating world,
a globe on which we stepped, duck-footed
carrying our cargo load — red bundle of laundry-looking bunting
up and down streets where teenaged boys
stepped out from New Year's parties to their cars
taking long steps, like timber wolves, and looked
at us, and in those always-surprisingly gentle voices
wished us a happy new year.

I was a ten year old child on New Year's Eve when death-terrors
        first struck —
all those people in Times Square celebrating
were going to die,
even the great Lombardo, and his band;
but worst of all myself, and everyone I loved —
hypo of terror like a salty wafer on my tongue,
burning the back of my head with fire —
but what is the use in hating time,
when everything we've ever loved is made of it?

I've always thought that we could live forever,
coming to terms with the tyrants who live in us.

I've always hoped that love would have the final word
and slowly, by accumulation, perhaps it will,
at first by a simple majority
—for anything learned by one is soon accessible to all
and if we could master the trick, with faith we could leap up &
     really touch the moon
and everything imaginable is real.

I'm not so sure about me
but you, little bear, must go on forever . . .
beautiful swimmer who sky-dived into time—
with your sweet-smelling skull as fragile as a china teacup
and your sleeping hands curled toward your heart,
with your raspy breath sawing to the center of the house
and the blue vein at your temple mapping a new country.
With your butterfly dreams of milk and motion,
your nose pressed in the flannel for the smell of the earth,
with your scruffy cradle-cap and feather hair blown in the wind
     from my breath,
with your neck that flops your heavy head from side to side to
     side
forty or fifty times before you settle finally into sleep,
your edible skin-scent and the two infinite parallel lines above the
     nail of your thumb.
Beauty and mystery here snoring softly at my side.

The year's first dawn floated from black to peacock blue stained
     glass of sky
through which I saw our neighbor's window freighted with snow,
and then day broke—gray-gold and violet-pink
—and you woke crying from your hunger for the world.

Li-Young Lee

A FINAL THING

I am that last, that
final thing, the body
in a white sheet listening,

the whole of me trained,
curled like one great ear on
a sound, a noise I know, a

woman talking
in another room,
the woman I love; and

though I can't hear
her words, by their voicing
I can guess

she is telling a story,

using a voice which speaks to another,
weighted with that other's attention,
and avowing it
by deepening in intention.

Rich with the fullness of what's declared,
this voice points
away from itself
to some place

in the hearer,
sends the hearer back
to himself
to find what he knows.

A saying full of hearing,
a murmuring full of telling
and compassion for the listener
and for what's told,

now interrupted by a second voice,

thinner, higher, uncertain.
Querying, it seems
an invitation to be met,
stirring anticipation, embodying
incompletion of time and the day.

My son, my first-born, and his mother
are involved in a story no longer only theirs,
for I am implicated,
all three of us now
clinging to expectancy, riding sound and air.

Will my first morning of heaven be this?
No. And this is not
my last morning on earth.
I am simply last
in my house

to waken, and the first
sound I hear
is the voice of one I love

speaking to one we love.
I hear it through the bedroom wall;

something, someday, I'll close my eyes to recall.

Acknowledgments

Ai: "The Mother's Tale" is from *Sin*. Copyright © 1986 by Ai. Reprinted by permission of Houghton Mifflin Company. All rights reserved.

Bennett, Gwendolyn B.: Much of Bennett's work appeared in the literary arts journals *Opportunity* and *Fire!!* (the latter of which she founded), published during the Harlem Renaissance. The place where "Secret" originally appeared has not been discovered.

Berryman, John: "Dream Song #129" is from *The Dream Songs*. Copyright © 1969 by John Berryman. Reprinted by permission of Farrar, Straus and Giroux, Inc.

Bloch, Chana: "Eating Babies" is from *The Secrets of the Tribe*. Copyright © 1980 by Chana Bloch. Reprinted by permission of Sheep Meadow Press.

Burkard, Michael: "A Raincoat" is reprinted by permission of the author.

Carruth, Hayden: "The Death" is from *Tell Me Again How the White Heron Rises and Flies across the Nacreous River at Twilight Toward the Distant Islands*. Copyright © 1989 by Hayden Carruth. Reprinted by permission of New Directions Publishing Corporation.

Clifton, Lucille: "the lost baby poem" is from *good woman: poems and a memoir, 1969–1980*. Copyright © 1987 by Lucille Clifton. Reprinted by permission of BOA Editions Ltd., 92 Park Avenue, Brockport, NY 14420.

Coleman, Anita Scott: While much of Coleman's work appeared in *The Crisis*, a literary arts journal published during the Harlem Renaissance, little is known about the details of her life. The date of her death and the place where "Black Baby" originally appeared have not been discovered.

Creeley, Robert: "Mother's Voice" is from *Mirrors*. Copyright © 1983 by Robert Creeley. Reprinted by permission of New Directions Publishing Corporation.

cummings, e. e.: "if there are any heavens my mother will (all by herself) have" is reprinted from *ViVa*, poems by e. e. cummings, edited by George James Firmage, by permission of Liveright Publishing Corporation. Copyright 1931, 1959 by e. e. cummings. Copyright © 1979, 1973 by the Trustees for the e. e. cummings Trust. Copyright © 1979, 1973 by George James Firmage.

Ginsberg, Allen: "Kaddish," sections III, IV, V, is from *Collected Poems, 1947–1980*. Originally published Harper & Row. Copyright © 1959 by Allen Ginsberg. Reprinted by permission of the author.

Gluck, Louise: "The Gift" and "Night Piece" are from *Descending Figure*. Copyright © 1976, 1977, 1978, 1979, 1980 by Louise Gluck. First published by The Ecco Press. Reprinted by permission.

Hadas, Rachel: "Up and Down" is from *Son from Sleep*. Copyright © 1987 by Rachel Hadas. Reprinted by permission of Wesleyan University Press.

Halpern, Daniel: "An Early Death" is from *Tango*. Copyright © 1987 by Daniel Halpern. Used by permission of Viking Penguin, a division of Penguin Books USA Inc.

Harper, Michael S.: "Lecturing on the Theme of Motherhood" is reprinted by permission of the author. "Mama's Report" is from *Debridement*, published by Doubleday. Copyright © 1972, 1973 by Michael S. Harper. Reprinted by permission of the author.

Hawley, Beatrice: "The Bad Mother" is reprinted from *The Collected Poems of Beatrice Hawley*. Copyright © 1989 by the estate of Beatrice Hawley. Reprinted by permission of Zoland Books, Cambridge, MA.

Hayden, Robert: "The Whipping" is from *Angle of Ascent: New and Selected Poems*. Reprinted by permission of Liveright Publishing Corporation. Copyright © 1975, 1972, 1970, 1966 by Robert Hayden.

Howes, Barbara: "2nd Wind" is from *A Private Signal: Poems New and Selected*. Copyright © 1977 by Barbara Howes. Reprinted by permission of Wesleyan University Press.

Hughes, Langston: "Mother to Son" is from *Selected Poems of Langston Hughes*. Copyright © 1926 by Alfred A. Knopf, Inc. and renewed 1954 by Langston Hughes. Reprinted by permission of Alfred A. Knopf, Inc.

Hugo, Richard: "White Center" is from *Making Certain It Goes On: The Collected Poems of Richard Hugo*. Reprinted by permission of W. W. Norton, Inc. Copyright © 1983 by the Estate of Richard Hugo.

Ignatow, David: "#34" is from *Shadowing the Ground* published by Wesleyan University Press. Copyright © 1991 by David Ignatow. Reprinted by permission of University Press of New England.

Jarrell, Randall: "The Truth" is from *The Complete Poems*. Copyright © 1944, 1949 and renewal copyright © 1971, 1976 by Mrs. Randall Jarrell. Reprinted by permission of Farrar, Straus and Giroux, Inc.

Strand, Mark: "Pot Roast" is from *The Late Hour*. Reprinted by permission of Atheneum Publishers, an imprint of Macmillan Publishing Company. Copyright © 1973, 1975, 1976, 1977, 1978 by Mark Strand. Originally appeared in *The New Yorker*.

Svoboda, Terese: "On My First Son" is from *All Aberrations* published by the University of Georgia Press. Copyright © 1985 by Terese Svoboda. Reprinted by permission of the author.

Tate, James: "For Mother on Father's Day" is from *The Lost Pilot*. Copyright © 1978 by James Tate. First published by The Ecco Press in 1982. "Distance from Loved Ones" is from *Distance from Loved Ones* published by Wesleyan University Press. Copyright © 1991 by James Tate. Reprinted by permission of University Press of New England.

Wakowski, Diane: "Poem for a Little Boy on the Buddha's Birthday" is from *Emerald Ice: Selected Poems 1962–1987*. Copyright © 1988 by Diane Wakowski. Reprinted by permission of Black Sparrow Press.

Waldman, Anne: "Complaynt" first appeared in *Helping The Dreamer* published by Coffee House Press. Copyright © 1989 by Anne Waldman. Reprinted by permission of the publisher.

Wheelwright, John: "And for His Mother" is from *Collected Poems*. Copyright © 1971 by Louise Wheelwright Damon. Reprinted by permission of New Directions Publishing Corporation.

Williams, C. K.: "My Mother's Lips" is from *Poems, 1963–1983*. Copyright © 1988 by C. K. Williams. Reprinted by permission of Farrar, Straus and Giroux, Inc.

Williams, William Carlos: "The Horse Show" is from *The Collected Poems of William Carlos Williams, 1939–1962, Vol. II*. Copyright 1949 by William Carlos Williams. Reprinted by permission of New Directions Publishing Corporation.